THE

FATHER'S
HORSE

A VISION TO TAKE US WHERE WE TRULY BELONG

MICHAEL FICKESS

BOOK THREE OF **THE GREAT ACCELERATION** TRILOGY

The Father's Horse
by Michael Fickess
Copyright © 2018
First Edition

Visit **www.michaelfickess.com** for a full list of resources,
timely prophetic words, media appearances, and more.

ISBN—978-1719064965; 1719064962

Cover Design: Michael Fickess
Layout/Illustrations: Michael Fickess
Editing: Edward Fickess

Table of Contents

"And what we have said is even more clear
if another priest like Melchizedek appears,
One who has become a priest not on the
basis of his ancestry but on the basis of
the power of an indestructible life."

—Hebrews 7:15-16, *emphasis added*

Introduction

It is no accident that I was given most of the revelation for this book on Father's Day weekend of 2017, for the primary message of this book is about our heavenly Father. I had just finished editing book two of *The Great Acceleration* series while riding in the car on a family vacation. I was not expecting to write the third volume for another year or two because I had other projects planned. However, something unique has been happening to me lately—it is like when I cut a zinnia flower in my garden and *two* grow up in its place. As soon as I clear a book from my threshing floor and think I am caught up, the Lord comes with a fresh revelation that is even more captivating to me than what came before.

One reason that authentic revelation is coming quickly to many in the Body of Christ right now is because *the time is short.* Jesus explained about His own ministry, **"As long as it is day, we must do the works of him who sent me. Night is coming, when no one can work" (John 9:4).** As followers of Christ, we must also keep working as long as the Lord gives us light. I have kept writing at a feverish pace because I am keenly aware that it will be much easier to bring forth these kinds of revelations before the midnight hour strikes. For when the midnight cry echoes out, it will be the darkest time in human history and only those who have *already* stored up oil will be ready to trim their lamps and shine.[1] My primary goal in sharing these revelations is to add to the weight and depth of oil that every saint is already carrying within themselves, so they will have a bright

---

[1] See the Parable of the Wise Virgins in Matthew 25.

vision of hope to share when the world is shaken by greater darkness.

The second reason revelation is coming to many people more quickly is the same reason the Lord is happy to give me additional zinnias in my garden—because He loves us and wants us to see the world as He does. It delights the Father when we become enraptured by the beauty the revelation He gives, just as it delights Him when we are enraptured by a delicate flower or a remarkable sunrise in His creation. This kind of simple, child-like delight and desire may be the most important attributes for us to cultivate in our spiritual lives because they open the door to everything else. This is why Jesus told us that we need to, **"receive the kingdom of God like a little child" (Mark 10:15).**

Many pastors and teachers give excellent teaching on the purpose of the prophetic, the different kinds of revelation we can receive, or how to interpret prophetic symbols. These are important concepts to learn if we are called to fulfill a prophetic calling. I too have created teaching grids, systems, and processes to help others identify and discern spiritual things.[2] However, if we think of spiritual gifts as mere tools to do a job, then we are stuck with a mechanical approach to a spiritual life, devoid of the child-like wonder we are meant to maintain. These concepts are important because this final installment in the series is focused on the kind of relationship with God the Father we are meant to have—a relationship that is driven deeper through desire, delight, and unrelenting obedience.

---

[2] See *Workbook 2* from the CSCL Bible Curriculum Series.

The Scope and Trajectory of this Series

If this is the first book in this series you have picked up, it can stand alone as a glimpse of the deeper walk with Father God to which we are all called. However, for the benefit of first-time readers or those who have not read this series in a while, a brief overview may be helpful. The first installment, entitled *The Great Acceleration,* gave a prophetic glimpse of some of the events that will accompany the great harvest of souls, including a time of rising darkness and the rise of a mature priesthood of believers with great authority over the darkness. The second installment, entitled *The Burning Cloud,* provided an in-depth view of how the Body of Christ will be taken higher in God so that each one can use their unique gifts to establish the kingdom of heaven on the earth.

The Burning Cloud called readers to a higher communion with God that is so real and tangible that it will be like when Moses and the seventy elders of Israel, **"ate and drank and saw God"** on Mount Sinai (see Exodus 24:11). However, since the book was primarily focused on the spiritual *tasks* God was calling us to complete, it did not fully address what it was really like to encounter the Father or how to access His intimate friendship in practical terms. This installment completes the series by fully elaborating on the theme of partnership and fellowship with the Father, a reality that was perfectly embodied in Christ's life. Although the calling to bring in the harvest and become a fully functioning spiritual priesthood are important, this book highlights an upward calling that outshines both of these things because it is the higher path of sweet communion with the Father we will traverse for all of eternity—long after every other task is finished.

The Circumstances of these Revelations

The specific circumstances in which we receive revelation can be important keys to help us understand it. Like the other books in this series, this installment came primarily through visions and was completed in the watches of the night as I sought the Spirit of Wisdom for interpretation and clarification. The bulk of this book came to me as a series of visions on the day I arrived in Nashville, Tennessee on the Friday before Father's Day weekend in 2017. I believe this detail is important because much of this revelation is about "the Father's horses" and I was staying in what some have called "horse country." Most of the visions took place a few hours after arriving in Nashville, when I went to the gym to workout. Although this may seem like a strange place to hear from the Lord, being there allowed me to be totally secluded in my thoughts and communion with God, uninterrupted from the social concerns of loved ones.

Although this prophetic allegory came as series of visions from the Spirit of God, it is important to emphasize that I consider it to be a *parable* that highlights biblical truths and promises. Just as revelations in scripture may either be literal or allegorical, there are some truths in this parable that are literal glimpses into the eternal realms, while others are mere symbols pointing to the truths of the scriptures. As a prophetic author, my primary job is to accurately scribe the revelation I am receiving. While I try to give interpretation where the Lord leads me to, I also trust my readers to interpret and apply these revelations by the same **"Spirit of wisdom and revelation"** that gave them to me (see Ephesians 1:17). It always excites me when readers share insights and interpretations about my prophetic allegories that go beyond what I saw when I wrote them.

I was only at the gym for an hour and twenty minutes when I arrived in Nashville. However, it felt like three or four hours because I scribed out much of what I was seeing during that time and began to compile it into this third manuscript of this series—and yet I still had time for a "back and bi's" workout. I am not sharing these details to brag, but to stir faith for what I call "time miracles," which happen when we are given the grace to transcend earthly time, either because we are planted in the eternal realms or we need additional time finish an assignment from the Spirit of the Lord.[3] This was not the first time this has happened to me. I wrote *Paths of Ever-Increasing Glory*—a 275-page book—in only two and a half weeks. Often when I am writing, the night watches feel *much longer* than the six or eight hours on the clock.

Although I normally do not share these kinds of stories because they are part of my personal history with God and some would not believe them, I am sharing these examples because one aspect of this series is a revelation about our relationship to time itself and I want to stir faith for others to begin having "time miracles" as we grow in deeper relationship with a God who transcends time. In each book of this series, the revelations often involve different aspects of

---

[3] See Ephesians 2:6, Colossians 3:1-3.

transcending time. For example, the characters may receive revelation from the past, the present, or the distant future— or even leave the limited domains of time and space to explore heaven's eternal shores. These elements of this trilogy point to a "theology of time" which is being restored to our generation as one aspect of our inheritance under the New Covenant. If you would like to explore the clear Biblical foundations for this "theology of time," I recommend my theological book, *Restoring the Apostolic Gospel,* which explains our relationship to time and eternity as one of the aspects of our New Covenant inheritance the Lord is restoring to us in this hour.

Thank you for supporting my writing gift with your purchase of this book. These books would not be possible without the loving support of my wife Rachelle, the helpful advice of my parents, and the intercessors who agree with me for breakthrough at each stage in the process. If the Holy Spirit touched your life through this series or other resources I offer, I would love to hear from you.

Many Blessings,

Michael Fickess

1 | The Resurgence of Memory

It was the furthest he had ever been from home. He was accustomed to walking with his father daily, discussing everything that happened. He relied on his wisdom, his guidance, his strong presence. If he was ever unsure of how to handle a situation or felt drained from the responsibilities he carried, he could always return to drink deeply from the cup of wisdom and love his father offered. He was moved with great love by so many things he encountered as he walked the dusty streets of Israel's small towns, but it was a love that flowed from what he stored up within himself from even longer walks with his father.

When he was with his father—sometimes in the cool of the morning before his close friends woke up and sometimes in the late evening as the watch fires burned—he always felt at home. It didn't matter if the weather was stormy or if there was conflict swirling around him. For his heart was always at home, completely wrapped in the strong love of his father. However, his father gave him much more than love and wisdom. His father shaped his identity, showing him who he was and where he really belonged. For in the solitary hours, when a deep quieting mist fell upon the land, washed in blue starlight, his father would come in the fullness of His Spirit, wrap himself around him, and restore the full awareness of who He really is. It was in these times that he was not merely told who He is, but he saw the truth clearly. And as the memory was restored with rising intensity, their relationship deepened all the more.

It was this returning and deepening memory of who he really was and who He was *before* that deepened their relationship, giving him the confidence to walk in greater authority. It was an authority rooted in relationship, an authority that flowed from simply *being* his father's son. As the cup of memories began to overflow with what *was* true and what *is* true, he began to move forward, to discover *what would soon be*—all that His father had in store for Him in the future. Even though these things had not yet happened, the revelations of his destiny felt like memories too, for they carried the same warmth and depth of experience as something that had already happened. It was a resurgence of memory not only from the distant past and from His place in the eternal realms before time began—but also from the future, when He would be seated in a place of all authority, matchless glory, and total supremacy. And the more He saw of what He would become in the future, the more He began to walk in it *now*.

The other kind of memory that was restored was the memory of who His Father was, is, and would forever be. For as He beheld each aspect of the Father's glory—His love, His compassion, His Wisdom, His full mystery—He encountered these attributes as something that is always true and never fails. For the Father had always loved Him, He loved Him now, and He would love Him forever. His Father imparted Wisdom about what was, what is, and is to come —as well as what was happening in hidden places far outside of time. So, it was that as He drew closer in relationship with His father, He began to stretch past the limitations of His earthen vessel with its limitations and discover who He truly was as He explored the deeper thoughts and desires of His Father. These revelations of the Father's **"higher thoughts"** and **"higher ways"** of living would crash over Him like a succession of golden waves, lifting Him ever higher until His own thoughts and desires matched His Father's.[4]

After thirty years of resurgent memories, He was ready. For the picture of His full identity was now imparted—an identity that encompassed all of time, all of eternity, and all of the Father's glory. He now began the short walk to his cousin John, who was baptizing in the Jordan. John had also been spending time with the same Father. As a prophet, John was also given glimpses of who Jesus was, is, and would become in the future. He also knew his family history well— He had heard about the angels that visited his own parents and the parents of Jesus, the star that drew the Magi from the East, the company of angels who proclaimed Jesus' birth, and the ancient prophecies detailing the circumstances of Christ's birth now fulfilled. But now as Jesus approached in the distance, the Spirit moved upon John with greater power than ever before and for the first time he too saw Jesus in the pure bright light of the heavenly Father's love. He did not merely perceive a cold, sterile view of his *role,* for he was now flooded with the Father's own thoughts and emotions about His most-loved Son.

---

4 See Isaiah 55.

"As the cup of memories began to overflow with what was true and what is true, he began to move forward, to discover what would be —all that His father had in store for Him in the future."

As John looked at Jesus drawing closer to the Jordan to be baptized, tears of love flowed down his face. For he could now see that, above all else, the Father deeply *loved* his son. He could feel the weight and depth of it churning inside of him and His head reeled from the revelation. But he could also see something more, for Jesus was walking in a level of the Father's manifest presence and power that no one had ever seen before. He could clearly see that Jesus now had the Spirit of God **"without limit,"** the full expression of the seven-fold Spirit of God reserved only for the Messiah.[5] Being a prophet, John could see it clearly—the seven burning flames all around Jesus—and he knew that his cousin had risen to a level of authority that made him unstoppable. He knew that while he was baptizing in water and **"preparing the way"** by preparing hearts and minds, *this man* would soon baptize people with the same **"spirit and fire"** that he now saw radiating from Christ's whole being.[6]

As Jesus began to step into the water, John felt unworthy to even touch him. As one who baptized people for repentance—bringing them out of sin and into a holy life— John was used to discerning the sin that people carried. When he baptized people with repentance, this gift of prophetic discernment would enable him to let them know if they forgot something. But when Jesus came, there was no sin to remind him of, no sin to wash away. Instead, his discernment gift enabled John to see Christ shining with the pure white light of holiness. John now felt like *he* needed to

---

[5] See John 3:34, Isaiah 11:1-2, Zechariah 3, Revelation 4.

[6] See Matthew 3:1-3, Matthew 3:11, Luke 3:16.

be baptized again—maybe even many times. For the love, power, and glory radiating from Jesus grew as He approached, until John's thoughts and emotions were overcome with the weight of it. He turned to his cousin with tears in his eyes and trembling hands and said,

"I need to be baptized by you, and do you come to me?"[7]

Having already seen what must happen today, Jesus spoke with confidence, **"Let it be so now; it is proper for us to do this to fulfill all righteousness."**[8] As he spoke, John could see the flames and feel the depth of the Spirit swirling around Christ. He knew better than to put up an argument. He led him to the central flow of the river over a wide flat stone outcrop in the water and dipped him under just as he had done to thousands of others. But as Jesus came out of the water, it was remarkably different from anyone else who had been baptized there—for the power and glory Christ carried now became visible to everyone present. First, the Spirit of God descended upon him as a soft light, as gentle and snowy white as a dove. But when the Spirit rested and remained on him, Jesus took on a much fiercer look, for He carried not only the full expression of gentleness and love, but also of truth and power and holy fear. It was the moment he was totally at home, the circle of golden communion with Father and Spirit complete—now the *three* were made one. Even though Jesus already knew He was loved by the Father, the Father now declared it

---

[7] See Matthew 3:14.

[8] See Matthew 3:15.

openly so that everyone else would know it. All those present now heard the thunderous voice from heaven declare: **"This is my dearly loved Son, who brings me great joy!"**[9] It was a proclamation of His true home—for the Son had learned to abide in the Father's love and live His life as an overflow of everything the Father showed Him daily.[10] That golden circle of unbroken communion with the Father was Christ's true home—and He knew that one day He would bring many more into it.[11]

But in the throbbing pain, that moment of baptism and declaration now felt like a lifetime ago. For this was now the farthest he had ever been from home. The violence had begun in Gethsemane, as he began to take upon himself every temptation, every shadow of darkness, every weakness known to man. The cup was so bitter, the inner turmoil so intense, that his sweat became mingled with drops of blood. As he progressed through betrayal, rejection by both the Jews and the Gentiles, flogging, torture, and mockery, he had felt further and further away. But the nails—

When the nails were driven into his hands, something beyond comprehension happened. For all of the transgressions of mankind were laid upon him in full force at that moment.[12] When the nails went in, a dark veil of separation fell between himself and the Father. With each pound of the hammer, he felt the Father's rejection and

---

[9] See Matthew 3:17 NLT.

[10] See John 5:19-20.

[11] See John 17.

[12] See Isaiah 53:6.

wrath come in throbbing waves of pain. He felt desperation instead of power, forsaken instead of loved. He could not look to his Father's face this time for sustenance and no angel came to his aid. He knew that six was the number of man and he was redeeming all of mankind, but he still had to go through the atonement process of hanging there for *six* full hours—naked, bleeding, and utterly forsaken by the Father. In his body and in his mind, time now came to a screeching halt. For He began to lose consciousness, but found no more solace in his dreamy state than when he was awake in the throbbing pain. The sky grew dark all around Jerusalem and he began to see the same creeping, soul-piercing darkness whether he closed his eyes or opened them.

Although he could no longer commune with the Father in this state, he was not spiritually *unaware*. In fact, he was more spiritually *aware* now than ever before. And so, he bore not only the sin, but the shadow of spiritual darkness that surrounds the heart of man like a death shroud.[13] He fell into a level of hopelessness that felt like a bottomless, cold, and stale chasm—with no water, no light, no breath of fresh air. Having already unleashed their cruel evil upon his body, the powers of darkness now taunted his heart and mind with cruel thoughts and crippling emotions. He reminded himself—yes, this shadow of darkness is part of the curse too. The onslaught of darkness piercing his soul was far worse than the nails now piercing his hands and feet.

---

[13] See Isaiah 25:7-8.

He remembered his cousin again and the words he spoke with tear-filled eyes as he saw his destiny:

"Behold, the Lamb of God, who takes away the sin of the world!" (John 1:29)

The Father had already shown him the great fruit that would be born from the tree he hung on now. He had shown him a glimpse of the heavenly Jerusalem at many stages throughout his life, the vast multitude of Jew and Gentile made holy, the holy nation that He himself had conceived of in the golden chamber of counsel with the Father and the Spirit before time began. Having had his memories restored, he knew that he had already weighed all of the wickedness of mankind against the love of the Godhead and *He* had decided, along with the Father and the Spirit—that love would win. And now this was the place that he would prove it. This is where He would remember and fulfill the judgement He made *against Himself* on behalf of mankind.

He did not lose His resolve, even in the face of the penetrating darkness. Although the pain was excruciating and the darkness pierced like sharp fangs through his heart and mind, **"not one of his bones was broken."**[14] He had consumed every resurgent memory, every revelation of the Father's glory, until it became woven into the fabric of his very nature—and the memory of the Father's glory was still there inside him now, as fire in his bones. Despite being forsaken by the Father now, as He bore the weight of man's

---

[14] See Psalm 34:20, John 19:36.

sin in heart, mind, and body, He could still lean back and remember the long hours of communion had become woven into the deepest parts of his nature as Son of Man. He could not look into the Father's present thoughts from this place, but He could still remember the ones he had looked into in the past, just as one remembers a favorite movie they have seen many times.

So, when the thief to his right turned his head and said, **"Jesus, remember me when you come into your kingdom,"** the Son of God could recall the memories of what he had seen in the golden chamber when he decided to pay the price to redeem mankind before time began (Luke 23:42). He remembered seeing this man and weeping for him in the long stretches of eternity before time began. And now, remembering with full presence of mind, he turned his head back and replied with confidence,

"Truly I tell you, today you will be with me in paradise" (Luke 23:43).

*The love, power, and glory radiating from Jesus grew
as He approached—until John's thoughts and emotions
were overcome with the weight of it.*

The Father's Horse

2 | The Father's Stables

Throughout all the long stretches of eternity, which reached back with unfathomable length, the Father had been pouring His love into His Son and into the Spirit. And in that same golden circle of communion, the Son and the Spirit had poured their love back into the Father. For their communion was an unbreakable circle of triune love, power, and glory. It was a communion so full of thought, emotion, and creativity that the angels could not restrain themselves from continual worship. When the communion of the Godhead[15] was focused on love for one another, or communicating other aspects of their own eternal nature to each other by revelation, the Seraphim and Cherubim would cry out—

**"Holy, holy, holy is the Lord God Almighty,
Who was and is and is to come!" (Revelation 4:8)**

In this way, the angels would worship the *nature* of God each time they perceived it. But when the thoughts of the Godhead turned towards the created order, the fall and redemption of man, a restored cosmos, or the holy city yet to rise from the ashes, the Seraphim and Cherubim would see the plan of redemption and call out to *each other*, as if

---

[15] **Godhead**—*a synonym for the Trinity which points to their supremacy*

mimicking the silent conversation of the Godhead about the coming waves of restoration—

"Holy, holy, holy is the Lord Almighty;
The whole earth is full of his glory!" (Isaiah 6:3)

Similarly, as each new revelation of the nature of God was declared, as each new thought from the Godhead was poured out in the golden chamber, the seven flames before the throne burned with vibrant color and power. It was as if these seven flames were a mirror, reflecting with perfection everything that was hidden in the heart of the Father and the Son.

But now, this was also the furthest *the Father* had ever felt from home. It was not only the Son who suffered in those six long hours of separation. For now, the Father also learned how painfully long an hour can be. And for the first time, the circle of golden light was broken. The Father had no place to invest the perfect love, glory, and power that he had continually poured into His Son for all eternity. Yet from his heart, the lightning continued to pour forth as a river of pure white fire, with no fit vessel to pour it into. Faced now with an agony of His own, he now walked through the garden of God, past a long grove of fruit and nut trees, and stopped at a long row of horse stables across from a vibrant green pasture. The sky was grey as if it had just rained and the vibrant green grass was well-trimmed and wet. For in the long hours of separation from his Son, the Father came to bless the horses.

The first stable he came to on the left as he walked down the path had two chestnut brown and white mustangs. The brown and white markings reflected the humility and holiness in which their riders had walked. Now they waited here until they were needed again. Sensing the Father's mood with what was happening below, they snorted and bucked at his approach, remembering their wild nature for a moment. The Father smiled at them, and looked back to the time and place he had brought them here, for their masters never experienced death. They had each come from different times and places, but both had won great victories against the powers of darkness in their times. Both had helped to prepare the way.

When they first came to this stable, they had needed the rest they were given. But now they were beginning to thirst for a new challenge again. The Father spoke to them now, "Peace!" When he said it, their rippling muscles stopped immediately and their ears turned to him.

"Everything your masters hoped for and believed for is about to come to pass now. Everything they saw will soon be fulfilled. You will be released again when you are needed and you will get one more chance to shine in battle. Now grow strong!"

When he said, "grow strong," he gave them a bucket of resurgent memories—it was a reminder of who they were, deeper mysteries of who the Father is, and what would soon come upon the earth. But the memories were not only for themselves—for they were also the `memories' of great holiness and breakthrough from a *future* generation of overcomers. These were buried at the bottom of the bucket so the two wild colts would have to discover things about themselves before they discovered things about those they would be sent to train when they stepped out again at the end of the age.[16] As the Father moved on to the next stable, I knew it would take a long time for them to consume all they were given to eat and they would probably look very different when the gate opened for them to go out again.

The next stable had an open pasture on the back side instead of a wall. The landscape was arranged in vibrant green hills, but ended abruptly with a wall of stars on a field of deep black sky. This stable was much larger and housed a great multitude of fiery horses, whose riders were also flames of fire. Whenever holy people in Israel, in any time or place of its history, called out for help to the God of Israel in a time of darkness, the horses would hear a sharp whistle and dive through the field of black sky and the wall of stars to help them. But now it was the Father who whistled to them.

They perked up their ears and came bounding in immediately—not only from the green hills, but from the other side of the black sky. The whistle continued to reverberate and shake the hills all around Jerusalem and they came back to him at full throttle, like an army of bottle rockets headed for a central point. When they were all returned and assembled, there were so many of them that you could no longer see the hills or the field of black at all. They looked like a massive wall of fire burning all along the fence posts at a great height, but the fence posts were not consumed and they did not cross the line they made.[17] I remembered the Father's promise to Israel, **"For I...will be a**

---

[16] See Revelation 11:1-15.
[17] See 2 Kings 6:8-23, Psalm 121.

wall of fire all around her, and I will be the glory in her midst" (Zechariah 2:5).

To my surprise, the Father blessed them with *deafness—*

"You will not hear their calls again until Jerusalem is destroyed by fire and her people are scattered."

But he also gave them a promise—

"When I rebuild Jerusalem and regather the exiles from all the nations, I will restore your hearing to be much greater than ever before and your flames will burn brighter. In those days, the whole multitude of you will go to them at the faintest whisper and you will have the power to confuse and vanquish all of their enemies."

He gave this assembly of fiery horses a bucket of scrolls. As they ate them, they grew in power, and wisdom, and fire —just as the prophets do when they eat the scrolls given to them. These scrolls gave them the strategies they would need for overcoming, but in a manner that brought the most embarrassment and humiliation to Israel's enemies. I knew when they were fully mature, they would not only have the power to win battles, but to laugh and ridicule their enemies as they fought them.

As he walked from stable to stable, the Father's burden for His Son's suffering was not lessening with each horse he blessed, but *increasing* in intensity. For even as he walked, every thought and emotion was drawn to His Son with increasing fire. Seeing His agony, I began to wonder why He had come here at all—until I remembered I still did not know the final destination of His stroll.

The next stable was filled with creatures with heads like lions. They oscillated in and out of dimensions and I thought I saw parts of many different creatures in them. They were clothed in a powerful armor that twinkled with flashes of lightning, all of which made them impervious to darkness. The father smiled on them and said,

"You are precious to me because you bring the atmosphere of heaven to earth. Eat and grow strong."

These horses were a company of powerful angelic heralds who brought revelation that propelled the kingdom of heaven through a long line of true prophets and holy people, which stretched from the beginning of time until the end. They were both terrifying and captivatingly beautiful, for they carried the beauty and power of true revelation from the throne. The Father gave them a bucket marked, *"THOSE WHO WILL COME IN THE FUTURE."* As they ate, the horses were satisfied by a weighty revelation about a multitude made holy, a great assembly who would rise in the end as they were consumed with the beauty, depth, and power of a life fully yielded to the Father. Those who will come in the future were empowered to traverse with the Father in the eternal realms when they chose and see the Father's glory with no limitation—but these weighty revelations tore through the things that bound them, penetrating through the deepest seat of their emotions as a lion tears His prey.

The Father stopped for a long time and watched them, the love and longing He felt for his Son rising all the more, because "those who will come in future" reminded Him of the most loved Son who was suffering *now*. He looked at the bucket for a while, comparing the future suffering of these holy people with the present suffering of His Son below. Only a few of these holy people asked for rescue, for most were so drunk with the revelation the Father gave them that they hardly noticed the intensity of their suffering. Many considered it a great honor to share in Christ's sufferings and gave themselves as willing martyrs. For this future company did not face the darkness from a place of abandoned desolation as Christ did—but they faced the darkness on earth with the full weight of communion with the Father continually bolstering their vision and elevating their perspective. After seeing their resolve and being satisfied with their connectioin to His Son, he continued his walk to the next stable.

The next stable he came to was filled with tall white war horses. These horses were well-muscled and of a massive size, and they were finely trained in dressage.[18] Each was fitted with golden dressings and bridles and was surrounded by many trainers working closely with each horse until it could do its job perfectly. One of the trainers came up to me, as if asking for help, and explained,

---

[18] According to the International Equestrian Foundation, *dressage* is considered to be the "highest form of horse training" and is judged according to the horse's training in a series of precise and pre-determined movements.

"The people always welcome the white war horses, but they hardly ever welcome the trainers who prepare the way. This is why the white war horses can never stay very long. If the Father didn't call them back, they would do great damage."

As he said this, I saw a war horse coming back in from the other side—the earthly domain—as its trainers ran to bring it in. Its eyes were fiery and it was fiercely bucking.

I turned to him and said, "It looks completely uncontrolled!"

The trainer spoke quickly and seemed angry. "It's what the people wanted—an *uncontrolled* move of God. But control from the spirit of man is not the same thing as proper training from the Spirit of God. What they don't realize is that anytime they reject proper training and discipline from the Spirit, they fall under the control of man by default. Proper training is the only thing that will allow these white war horses to go throughout the earth. Every move of God that does not learn to yield to the bit and bridle of the Spirit will end quickly. We have enough trainers in heaven—we need more of them on earth if there is to be a move of God that will not end this way."

Our conversation over the fence ended abruptly as seven thunders erupted with such force that they shook all of the landscape around us, as well as the earth below. I remembered that where the Father went, His Spirit went too. The Father took a small scroll out of his shirt pocket and held it up. The scroll was no bigger than a stick of chapstick, yet the full strength of the seven thunders went into it until it began to hum and glow with power.   He motioned for the young trainer to come and gave it to him, whispering, "Eat and grow strong." As He said it, the Father placed his hand on his back, both in reassurance and to strengthen his backbone.

As the trainer nibbled off a small piece, he tumbled to the ground like a dead man. The Father stooped down low to place the remainder of the scroll in the bucket, as if to show the value of it. I remembered that the full measure of the seven-fold Spirit of God is invested even in the small inner witness that every believer is given. The small size of the scroll pointed to the small impressions the Spirit gives unbelievers—for these small impressions are what become our bit and bridle, enabling us to carry great power in the earth through our obedience to the Spirit on every matter.

After depositing the small scroll in the bucket, the Father hung a golden plaque over the stable where all the trainers and horses could see it. It gave clear instructions:

EVERY HORSE AND TRAINER MUST BE
TRAINED TO HEAR MY WHISPER.

When the trainers looked at the plaque, they could see every trainer who had come before and completed their task on the other side because they had known the Father's whisper and obeyed it. It was a constant reminder of their primary key to success. But when the Father looked at the plaque, he was reminded of his Son, who had obeyed every whisper and now suffered below. The love and glory he usually poured into his Son at this time of day continued to flow without ceasing. Yet it was beginning to spill out, as water behind a dam laps across the top of it just before it breaks. His unrestrained desire needed an outlet and He looked down the line of stables towards His destination.

He passed the next stable very quickly. It had four horses of different colors. They all looked like they were starving and the Father refused to feed them even a scrap. I realized it was because *they fed on each other* and never looked to him for anything. They were horrifying creatures and I wondered why the Father would keep them in his stables at all. The white horse in this stable was the worst-mannered horse I had ever seen. It had gold trimmings like the white war horses, but they were becoming a putrid green as the gold which only formed a thin layer on them was revealed as counterfeit. It was stronger than the other horses, so it continually bullied them, knocked them over, and pushed their faces into the dust. The red horse looked like it had rabies. It lashed out and bit the other horses, its eyes full of desperate fire. It was filled with equal measures of hatred and fear, both of which consumed it from the inside and drove it to lash out all the more. Any time a blade of grass grew along the fence line of this stable, the black horse would run to it and consume it immediately. In this way, all the horses in this stable became increasingly desperate to feed on *something*—which included anything or anyone they could find. The fourth horse was a sickly green color. He continually vomited in the stall and then returned to eat his own vomit. Each time he vomited, it smelled worse than before and soon *all* of the four horses in this stall began to grow sick from the stench of it.

The Father kept walking ahead at a fast pace, but I lingered for a moment to look more carefully at these four horses of *lust for power, famine, war,* and *pestilence.*[19] I felt a presence next to me and realized the three apprentices had joined me at this stable. The apprentice named *Eternal Wisdom* spoke first—

"They aren't his horses, but they are penned up here because he is the only one able to restrain them. They will only be fully released from this place after they have grown to their full strength."

"Why doesn't he just put them out of their misery?" I lamented.

Wisdom from the Past now explained, "He gave dominion of the earth to mankind. As long as sin remains, these curses will remain too. Throughout all of history, when man has become more wicked and godless, these cursed horses have fed upon their wickedness and grown stronger, bringing evil in the earth closer to maturity. But in the times and places when mankind chooses righteousness, justice, and wisdom, then these horses are penned up again. The horses cannot reach their full destructive potential until mankind—their rider—reaches the full maturity of evil."

I thought about the worst atrocities of the twentieth century and the challenges of today, but I still resented that these things were allowed to happen on the earth, even if mankind willed it to happen. Still unsatisfied, I protested,

---

[19] See Revelation 6, describing the four horsemen of the apocalypse which will be released in the end times.

"But why must they go throughout the earth and terrify mankind? Why has history been covered with such a deep shadow of darkness? Why does he allow the innocent to suffer? Why must things get *darker* in the end?"

Now *Wisdom from the Future* stepped closer and began to speak as a third witness—

"The full curse of sin must be brought into the light so that it can be properly identified, judged, and banished once and for all. These horses and their riders *must* mature—and be seen for what they are—before the end so that mankind will see why God's wrath against all wickedness, sin, and godlessness is completely justified. There is a reason these horses will be released just before the last judgement, for everything they do in the earth in that time will be a testimony *against* the wickedness of man and the powers of darkness so the case can be made for all manner of evil to be fully removed once and for all. In fact, if these four horsemen did not mature and go throughout the earth, then the restoration of all things and the banishment of the darkness could not take place. But take heart! The restoration of all things that is coming will far outshine anything that is lost."

Wisdom from the Past gave one last word— "Have you already forgotten what you have just seen? At the same time these four evil ones will come to maturity, the white warhorses that bring awakening, revival, restoration, and reformation will come to maturity as well. Both the white war horses and their riders are being whisper-trained in a manner that will make them unshakeable and invincible as they go throughout the earth.   Even if the trainers are martyred, the horses will only increase in power for in the last move of God, they will rely more on the Father's whisper for guidance than on any teacher or leader in the Body of Christ. This is why some of the greatest advancement of the kingdom in the last days, even *as* the four horsemen are doing their worst damage."

As he spoke, several flaming arrows came flying into the stable. The sickly horse was hit and greatly wounded and fell to the ground with a thud. I wondered if he was dead. Next, the deceptive white horse was hit right in the head with a flaming arrow, which caused him to temporarily forget his quest to take every mind captive. The red and black horses were hit with flaming arrows too. They reeled from the pain but did not fall completely. I looked back at the three apprentices for an explanation. They were all smiling and *Wisdom from the Past* began to talk quickly and with excitement.

"The remnant in the Body of Christ is beginning to discover how much power and authority they have. Every time they release a fiery arrow of unified prayer, prophetic declaration, or high praise, they are given additional days, weeks, months, and years to prepare for the harvest and bring it in. These arrows do not kill these four horses, but they slow down their progression through time and weaken them considerably. If it were not for these arrows going forth continually throughout the eighteenth, nineteenth, and twentieth centuries, the four horsemen would have already matured and gone throughout the earth. Just as mankind can empower these horses' destruction with godlessness and wickedness, mankind can stunt their growth or slow their approach by using living in righteousness and praying with authority."

His words were interrupted by a piercing cry from the last stall along the fence line which stood alone and up on a hill. It sounded like a wounded animal crying out in pain and it was a horrifying sound to hear. I ran ahead and left the three apprentices behind.

The plaque read—"EVERY HORSE AND TRAINER MUST BE TRAINED TO HEAR MY WHISPER."

The Father's Horse

3 | The Father's Horse

As I ran to the last stall, I could hear the cries of the wounded animal ringing out and echoing down the hill. As the pitiful cries cascaded down, it was like listening to a wounded child crying, *"Help me, father!"* repeatedly. The sound arrested me and brought my thoughts and emotions to attention.

As I approached the stall, the Father was doing something I had never seen Him do before. He was sitting on the rocky soil, holding the horse's head in his lap and weeping over it. The horse was in pitiful condition—its hair was torn out in wide patches which bled profusely. Although I suppose this horse had once been white, its hair was now so caked with blood and dirt so that it already looked like a corpse. The flesh along its torso was torn so deeply that you could see through the sliced-open muscle where the whips had torn all the way to the bone.

The horse cried out continually, *"Why, Father? Why? Why?"* For it remembered the times when they would trot together across the countryside. And now the Father remembered too—the long walks through deserts and mountains, resting in open pastures to consider the stars at night, and trotting through the small towns of Israel. The Father held the horse close to his chest and wept over it. As he did, it began to rain over the whole landscape in steady drops. His love rose in him now like a tsunami of pure white lightning ready to strike, but the Father's love could only release itself through tears of affection as he cradled the horse. Yet, there was no way for the horse to feel his emotion, for the pain and shadow of darkness on the horse was like a dark wall preventing the Father's love from breaking through to the other side. So as the Father loved all the more, the horse now writhed in pain. Nonetheless, the Father's horse still carried the love from their journeys together. Even in its writhing pain and suffering, the horse forgave those who had wounded it, if only to send the message to the Father across the dark chasm of separation,

"I haven't forgotten. The memories you gave me are still here and I am still who you have made me to be, even in the face of piercing darkness..."

The Father also wept because the horse had just returned from the only journey he had been asked to travel alone. It was a journey he knew would go through the darkest places in the heart of man and the cruelest hatred of the powers of darkness. However, these were only part of the journey. Even death itself was only part of the journey for the Father's horse—and not the final destination.

When the horse gave his last, loud cry, a great silence fell over all of the stables. Every horse and trainer, every worker in the Father's household, now listened attentively and the air felt pregnant with possibility. I looked back and the four horses were laying on the ground as though dead, for they were rendered completely powerless by the last cry of the Father's horse. The last cry of the Father's horse struck them like 10,000 flaming arrows launched together.

After the horse gave its last breath, the Father stood up and spoke to him, *"Holiness has given you the power of an indestructible life!"* The horse rose immediately to its feet but it did not yet take a breath. The Father spoke again, *"Holiness has given you the power of an indestructible life!"* The flesh was restored and the hair grew back pure and white and began to billow in a steady breeze but the horse still did not breathe. He spoke a third time, *"Holiness has given you the power of an indestructible life!"* Then a great wind went out from the Father and the breath of life now entered the horse again. It opened its eyes and remembered what it had been through. But the Father was not done yet. He now placed His hands on the horse and restored the memory of all they had walked through together, all that was, all that is, and all that must now be done. When he placed his hands on his horse, the dam broke and the Father imparted all of the love and wisdom and holiness and power He had held back. It came as a steady stream of pure white lightning which flowed into the horse. But the restoration of the horse also included revelations that had never been revealed by the Father until this hour—instructions that would carry it from victory to victory until every purpose of the Father was fully accomplished. The horse began to shine with a level of wisdom and power and love that terrified every power of darkness for it was now equipped to ride with the Father again, not only through heavenly places and neglected places on the earth, but to the low places where the captives of darkness awaited their deliverance from the curse of the Fall.

The Father drew a great lightning sword from His side now and fastened its hilt securely to the saddle of the white horse. He instructed it, "Go with haste!" and the horse jumped through a field of black stars and into the world below.

He instructed it, "Go with haste!" and the horse jumped through a field of black stars and into the worlds below.

The Father's Horse

4 | Journeys through Sheol and Hell

As he drew closer to his last breath, Jesus remembered all that the Father had shown Him. He remembered who He *had been*, who He *was,* and also who He *would become* after His last breath. He knew that his death signified the end of sin and the end of the curse of the fall. He knew that His death laid the foundation for a spiritual priesthood to rise in the future, with far more power than anything that came before. And so, with full knowledge that He was removing the curse of the fall once and for all, He cried out in a loud voice—**"Tetelestai!"**

The angels knew it was a declaration that the price of sin, which is death, was now paid in full.[20] The people who heard it knew that it was the seal placed on every contract, after the debt was paid in full. But this time, the earth heard it too. The hills around Jerusalem shook, not as a mere earthquake, but as if *something was coming.* As the quaking increased, it began to take on a steady rhythm, like great hooves pounding the earth and drawing closer.

And yet, the Son was sinking deeper and deeper into the darkness of death, falling to the place where dead men's souls

---

20 "Tetelestai!" means "It is finished!" or "Paid in full!"
See John 19:30, Matthew 27:50-54.

are continually tortured and oppressed by the powers of darkness in the places of hell called *Gehenna* or *Sheol*. These were like stone chambers in the earth where men were held until their redemption price was paid and now the Son found himself falling *past them*, going even deeper into the earth. He passed them and continued down past the angels who held the plates of the earth together, as well as the ancient powers of darkness who sought to disturb them, and kept falling, as one with no strength. He now reached the darkest council chambers of hell, where great treasures were held in captivity and the bodies of holy people were held on display with plaques that detailed all that the powers of darkness had done to harm them. He fell still deeper until he found the fallen angels meeting together in their dark counsel, drinking out of wine goblets and celebrating their victory that day.

But as the Son fell into deeper and deeper darkness, the horse released by the Father now chased after Him, clothed with all the memories and power and love He carried. Equipped with its terrible lightning sword and a revelation of what was to come (which the powers of darkness did not know), the Father's horse now galloped at full force, and each level of hell violently shook as the horse descended. Just as the Son reached the deepest pit of darkness and plunged the full depth of the abyss, the white horse came to Him, declaring the Father's words with the Father's distinct voice and His tone of love and longing, *"Holiness has given you the power of an indestructible life!"* The Son recognized it as His Father's horse, a remembrance of all the time they had spent together. He noticed it looked different now and he reached out to grab its reins. The horse repeated the Father's words again, *"Holiness has given you the power of an indestructible life!"* and the Son regained his strength and his wounds were healed, all except for the scars—which remained as an eternal testimony of what He had suffered. The horse repeated a third time— *"Holiness has given you the power of an indestructible life!"* and this time the Son breathed in all of the pent-up love, glory, and wisdom the Father had sent to Him. As a river of pure white lightning filled every aspect of His nature with fresh revelation form the Father, His sorrow was replaced with the laughter of victory and He reached down to grab the lightning sword which the Father had securely fastened to the saddle. For the Father's horse *was* the embodiment of the **"Spirit of Holiness"** that raised Jesus from the dead and declared Him to be the Son of God (see Romans 1:4).

The Son now leapt upon the horse, gripped its reins securely, and began a glorious upward journey. He mocked every power of darkness on His way up and showed them what they did not know—that every victory they had celebrated had become their certain defeat.[21] His lightning sword turned their victory cups into poison cups of woe and they were now rendered powerless in accordance with whatever measure they had drunk from them.[22] Yet, having purchased the right to completely remove all of them from the face of the earth, the Son left them there, frozen and stupefied by what was unfolding, so that a future generation might share in the delight of His victory, a generation who would learn to drink from the Father's love and glory in the

---

[21] See 1 Corinthians 2:8.

[22] See Isaiah 51:21-23.

same manner He did so that *their own horses* might be trained to relish the rigors of war.[23] As the horse galloped and brought the Son higher, the horse whispered with excitement,

"So he will sprinkle many nations, and kings will shut their mouths because of him! For what they were not told, they will see, and what they have not heard, they will understand" (Isaiah 52:15).

The Son saw at that moment how the Father had reserved the full and final victory over the powers of darkness for His mature sons and daughters to execute. He saw the armies that would follow in His wake and learn to identify, bind, banish, and judge the powers of darkness until they were completely banished from all of creation. He knew this victory *had* to be finished by mature sons and daughters in Christ, because only then would it last permanently. It was the new revelation the Father gave the horse to bring Him so that He'd have it at the precise moment he needed it.

As he rose to Sheol, the spirits of holy people were waiting in excited anticipation. Some had been waiting for decades, some for centuries, and some for millennia. Each had died *looking forward* in faith to the coming Messiah. Each had chosen to lay every hindrance aside and walk with God, often making great sacrifices as forerunners in the early millennia of the kingdom's advancement. Now, Christ approached, proclaiming a message He had fully internalized: *"Holiness has given you the power of an*

---

[23] See Jude 1:14-15, Revelation 19:11-21.

indestructible life!" Each time he said it, a third of Sheol was opened up and the bodies of holy people broke out of their graves, their bodies were now fully restored and glorified and their breath of life returned.[24]   When they emerged from Sheol, they came forth with **"all the powers of the age to come"**—although they had physical bodies, they could vanish if they chose, move at the speed of thought, and commune with the Father in the same manner that the Son did.[25]

When the Son reached Jerusalem, it was time to declare a new era and speak out the blessing of His resurrection over all of humanity. He saw a series of visions of restoration that guided His declarations over humanity.   First, He saw with greater clarity than ever before how the *heavenly Jerusalem* that would rise from the ashes of this earthly city. In the wake of the destruction soon to come, and the scattering of the Jews that would follow, He looked millennia into the future and saw a Body of Jews and Gentiles grafted together to be one holy nation and one holy priesthood, fashioned to see the Father face to face, in the same unbreakable circle of pure love that He enjoyed with the Father and the Spirit of Holiness.   And so, he now spoke over Jerusalem: *"Holiness has given you the power of an indestructible life!"* When he said it, he could see the horses of fire gather the exiles of Israel and bring them back in the future. He could see the nation reborn in the future. In the farthest mists of this age, He could see the great influx of Jews and Gentiles gathering to worship together at the Feast of Tabernacles.

---

[24] See Matthew 27:45-55.

[25] See Hebrews 6:5.

Next, He fixed His eyes on a mature priesthood that would rise in the future, a priesthood who would become a solid bridge between heaven and earth.   He called this priesthood out to do its job and saw their progression towards maturity over the next few millennia. When he saw them coming in the future, He declared over them again: *"Holiness has given you the power of an indestructible life!"* When he said it, the Father's horse stomped his foot repeatedly and the land shook violently. The furnishings of the temple which only served as a shadow of what was to come now toppled over, the burning incense caught things on fire, and the brass pipework that drained the blood from every sacrifice that foreshadowed him was ruptured and rendered unusable.

He fixed his eyes on a new vision the Father had given Him, a vision of every tribe, tongue, and nation made holy —of people from every family and every bloodline being grafted into the holy nation and holy priesthood.[26] As he saw it, he drew the horse slowly through the temple towards the veil, the curtain that hid the Father's glory from all of mankind. It was a symbol of the curse of the fall, the stain of sin that allowed the powers of darkness to misrepresent the Father and turn men's hearts away from him. He raised His lightning sword and tore it asunder, removing the veil of separation once and for all, on the basis of the curse He himself bore for all of mankind. Now he dismounted the horse for a moment and put on His priestly garments. He walked into the Most Holy Place and placed his hand on the center of the Ark of the Covenant, transmitting the blood

---

[26] See Revelation 7:9.

He had shed as one passes a modern security checkpoint with a fingerprint or retina scan. It was a door that only *He* could unlock. As soon as the blood was applied, a channel of unbroken fellowship with the Father was restored to Him —and to all who would be found *in Him* through faith in His finished works.

He needed the horse no longer, for He could now look into the Father's face again as one greets the morning light with joy. And now the love and glory of the Father filled Him with fresh lightning, a full awareness of *what would come.* He stretched out his hands towards all of humanity throughout all of time as their High Priest and proclaimed over them, *"Holiness has given you the power of an indestructible life!"* It went out through all of time as an invitation to leave the darkness and come into His ever-increasing light, glory, and fellowship with the Father.

When He said it, a lightning bolt of revelation rippled through all of space and time. Across different times and places in the past, the forerunners who preceded Him were awakened and filled with the light of His blessing. The apostles, prophets, and faithful reformers of every generation who would come in the future were similarly raised up and filled with the light of His blessing. And every move of God —leading right up to the final generation who would witness His return—were raised up by the light of His blessing. But because the light of His blessing also went out as an *invitation,* the greatest measure of revelation, holiness and power filled those in the final generation who would respond to His invitation with great desire.

The Father's Horse

5 | New Stables and Fresh Pastures

After blessing all of mankind from the Most Holy Place *on earth,* the Son ascended like lightning to the Most Holy Place in heaven. The blood was already on the mercy seat there, for it only needed to be applied once. But now, the Son came to the seven burning flames and looked through them, scanning the entire cosmos from beginning to end. He looked to the most distant nebulae, now clouds of fading dust—once destined to birth new stars, but now exploded from the weight of the curse of the fall. He looked to uninhabited planets and the farthest reaches in the heavens and into the different realms of heaven. And now, He spoke over all of the created order, on the basis of the blood He shed,

"Holiness has given you the power of an indestructible life!"

When he spoke it, the black field between the stars in all the cosmos brightened to a shining turquoise. As this happened, the stars brightened to be many thousands of magnitudes brighter and the planets at the farthest reaches, which looked like smoldering rocks that could hold no life, now became habitations for the saints to explore and cultivate in all the ages to come. He smiled with delight as the Father approached. When they embraced, every other thing seemed to vanish in the power of the golden light, for the circle of love was now restored. Now, the seven golden flames rose in much greater power than ever before and I knew that the level of love, glory, and power transmitted between them had risen *beyond* anything that had ever existed beforehand.

When they finished their embrace, the golden light dissipated and they were standing again in the pasture where the Father's horse had been just one day earlier, broken and unable to rise. With tears of love still in His eyes, the Father said,

"Now let us raise up new stables, new pastures, and a great army of horses to terrify the powers of darkness."

Having already seen the Father's plans as they embraced, the Son took the saddle and bridle off of the Father's horse and sent the Father's horse back out to pasture to rest for a while, soak in the saturating light and rain of heaven, and grow in size and strength.

The Son took the saddle in his hand and, holding it firmly, began to slice off one piece at a time from the saddle with a small pocketknife. As he cut off little pieces, no larger than a postage stamp, he threw them up into the air. As each piece slowly descended, it grew into a majestic war horse, each carrying a different truth that the Father had

"The chariots of God are tens of thousands and thousands of thousands; the Lord has come from Sinai into his sanctuary."—Psalm 68:17

revealed to His Son. As the Son worked on disassembling different parts of His own saddle, the horses took on different colors and were equipped for different tasks. The horn of the saddle became a series of blood-red horses—the embodiment of the message of the apostolic gospel which would be released with great power, first to birth the church, and again during the end times to bring it to maturity. Some horses came forth as great winds and carried their riders into uncharted waters as they restored important blueprints for higher worship, intercession, and communion with God. Others came forth clothed in the armor of pure light, embodying those who learned to faithfully use their gifts to glorify Christ, walk in love, and evangelize the regions they stood over in prayer.

Next, the Son took the bridle and threw it into the air. As it descended, it formed an army of terrifying war horses clothed in an impenetrable armor. These were for the saints of the final generation who were destined to judge and banish the powers of darkness from the earth. When these horses were revealed, they each had a terrifying chariot of lightning behind them. Even though the war horses themselves waded in to confront the darkness, those drawn by the chariots would ride in their wake, impervious to the influence of those they defeated in battle.

Since the Father and Son were in the *eternal* realms, all of the horses they released as portions from the saddle of the Father's horse went out into different slices of space-time, to the very people who were crying out for their full inheritance in Christ. From this one event, the whole trajectory of church history, of renewal and revival and a millennias-long march of the restoration of truth was released. But there was something more, for the Son of God did not sprinkle His blood over the earth alone, but over the Most Holy Place, the seat of government for the entire Cosmos throughout all of space and time. And so, when He divided the saddle, the portions were not only sent to release restoration in the years between now and his return, but they were sent out to all of the long stretches of eternity, to bring an ever-increasing and ever-expanding glory that would continue to release greater levels of the golden circle of love between the Father and Son over all of the cosmos forever.

I was reminded of the prophetic promise concerning what Christ had just done—

"The chariots of God are tens of thousands and thousands of thousands; the Lord has come from Sinai into his sanctuary.

When you ascended on high, you led captives in your train; you received gifts from men, even from the rebellious—that you, O Lord God, might dwell there" (Psalm 68:17-18).

As I meditated on this text later on, I thought it was strange that it said Christ had "*received* gifts from men," when He was actually *giving* them. Then I realized that as the only righteous Son, He had received the inheritance of the Father's love and glory and power that was in His heart for every nation, every tribe and every family line. He had received all of our gifts as an inheritance from the Father. And yet now, having purchased the right to restore all things,

He graciously gave it back to all of mankind—*one portion at a time.*

6 | Sending Out New Horses

His Body now raised from the dead with power by the Spirit of Holiness, Christ moved among the people with all the powers of the age to come. Although he possessed a *physical body* that bore real scars, although he could eat and his sandaled feet could still collect dust as he walked Israel's streets, He was now so unified with the Spirit of Holiness that when the Spirit moved, He moved. When the Spirit received instructions from the Father, that the Son of God should be hidden from human sight, or go here or there, He would vanish in a flash and reappear where the Father willed Him.

And so, he walked alongside them on the road to Emmaus in a different form.[27] He could see their hearts were disappointed and he was reminded of how *he* felt on the cross, as he was divorced from the golden circle of communion with the father. He remembered what it was like to be abandoned, confused, and momentarily blinded to the illuminating light of the Spirit. And so, he began to exhort and teach them everything they needed to know. He poured into them an encouragement and strength that come by properly seeing the total supremacy He accomplished

---

[27] See Luke 24:13-27 for the full description of this event.

through His death, resurrection, and ascension.[28]   But he could not resist giving them a bit more—for He could see they were hungry for more. So, he also began to reveal to them who *they* would become when the Holy Spirit came in power. As he spoke, their hearts burned within them for they could begin to glimpse a foreshadow of the golden circle of light soon to envelope them and draw them higher.

They continued on towards a home that offered hiddenness and safety from their persecutors, but at a fork in the road, the Lord started to walk down a different path in order to test them. Seeing his retreat and feeling the light begin to pull away from them, they now begged him, **"Stay with us, for it is nearly evening; the day is almost over" (Luke 24:29).** It was strange, but as they talked with this man who knew the scriptures so well, a love had grown in their hearts for Him so that, even after only an hour-long walk, they felt they might have known him forever.

As the sun was setting, the Lord raised his hands and thanked the Father for the food, but also blessed everyone in the room with a priestly blessing. They knew that no other man would release a *priestly blessing* at dinner time. As he blessed the food and blessed them, the weight of love and glory that flowed between Himself and Father flashed around them in the room. Suddenly, they could see Him *as the Father saw Him.* The atmosphere of the room changed and all eyes turned to Jesus. They could sense the Father's love for Him, but also the great holiness, wisdom, and power He carried. They now looked at his hands and saw the scars

---

[28] See Colossians 1.

from the nails and began to weep tears of joy. It was then that He vanished again in a flash of light, for the Father's desire called Him elsewhere.[29]

When he vanished, he left two blood-red horses behind. They breathed fire and sparkled with the powers of the age to come. They spoke in tongues and prophesied. They could breathe on any sick person and they would be restored immediately. They could open their mouths to proclaim the gospel and the Spirit would give the precise words to illuminate the scriptures and call people into deep repentance. Wherever the horses set their hooves, a deep imprint would be left from then until the Lord returned. Churches and movements of the Spirit followed in their wake. But the two who walked on the road to Emmaus could not see them yet or discern their presence. So, they did what men *without* horses do—they ran all the way to Jerusalem to tell the other apostles, as well as hundreds of men, women, and children who were hiding in various homes and villages for fear of their persecutors. As they ran, the red horses followed them unseen every step of the way.

It happened again while the two apostles were talking with the others, still out of breath from their journey. With tears of joy and love, they poured out their story. Even without seeing Jesus, the apostles knew that everything they said was true, for the same golden light that was on Christ's words, the light that flowed from deep relationship with the Father, was now carried upon their simple testimony. They couldn't see it with their eyes, but they could sense the deep

---

[29] See Luke 24:31.

truth in their words. And their eyes were beginning to open to a new bright dawn after what felt like a long winter's night.

As they spoke, the two blood-red horses stood by, stamping their feet and snorting. They were ready to get to work. But when the Lord appeared, the horses drew back because the intense light of His glory was overpowering and they wanted to watch what would happen next. The disciples were terrified when the Lord appeared in a flash of light. No yet having any frame of reference for the powers of the age to come, they reached for what they *could* understand. The Lord read all of their thoughts as they rose in their hearts and minds and spoke them back to them—

"Why are you troubled, and why do doubts rise in your minds? Look at my hands and my feet. It is I myself! Touch me and see; a ghost does not have flesh and bones, as you see I have" (Luke 24:38-39).

Seeing the scars on His hands and feet, half of them now believed. When they turned their hearts and joined the two other apostles in faith, six more blood-red horses stepped out of the golden pastures of heaven and into the realms below. I didn't know that horses could smile, but these horses were filled with the same joy their future masters had. They also had different qualities. One could gallop at the speed of light from city to city and the one who rode it would never be bound by space or time. One could look right into the third heaven and see the Father and the Son glorified—it was a level of prophetic revelation not seen on the earth in a very long time, but which was about to be restored. Another had important blueprints for developing the theology to save Gentile nations. I remembered that each horse carried a different portion of Christ's saddle—that each gift was a different portion of His mantle.

The Lord looked through the golden mists and saw the blood-red horses the apostles couldn't see. They weren't all there yet because they did not all believe. So, he kept pushing. He said with a clever smile, **"Do you have anything to eat?"**[30] They gave him a piece of broiled fish. He took it and ate it slowly, chewing and swallowing every bite so they could watch it go down. As he swallowed the second bite, another apostle believed in full and another blood-red horse trotted into the room.

After these simple demonstrations, the Lord now began to speak and allowed the full weight of the golden light from His communion with the Father to saturate His words. He taught them for an hour, explaining how the prophets had seen everything He would suffer, in addition to His resurrection, His supremacy, and the advancement of the kingdom in all the earth. A few of them were taking notes and adding them to vast stacks of notes they had already been compiling, eye-witness accounts of everything He had said and done among them for the last three years. It was when they were writing these notes that more of the blood-red horses stepped out of the golden mists—there were now eleven of them. I knew these horses that just came in would remain for a long time, guarding over these notes and ensuring that they would remain as eye-witness accounts

---

[30] See Luke 24:41.

forever.   These horses were equipped with the power of *memory* and they empowered the note-takers to remember everything Jesus had said and done.   But they were also crafty and knew how to hide the notes from the eyes of the enemy so they could not be destroyed before they were published for the nations.

And so, there were two assemblies there that day.   The apostles—and their *horses.*   Jesus took one more look at the horses and then gave the apostles some final instructions before vanishing again:

"I am going to send you what my Father has promised; but stay in the city until you have been clothed with power from on high" (Luke 24:49)

The horses stamped their feet with anticipation and the fire in them churned and flashed in their eyes.   They could hardly wait for the day to arrive—the day when the riders would recognize the gifts of power and angelic help they were given, the day when the apostles would step into the golden circle of love between Father and Son and take on all of the favor, power, and authority of the one and only Son. A day they would begin to live as Christ did because they would be positioned *in* the most-loved Son.   No matter how much they stamped their feet or snorted, no matter how much holy fire they conjured, they could not bring the day any closer.   But they were still missing one.

The other disciples, who had each seen the Lord, either on the road to Emmaus or in the room in Jerusalem were also joined by the women who had met Jesus at the garden tomb. They brought something to the group of men that was far deeper than any of the men could yet carry. It was a revelation from the living Christ about the very nature and substance of His Father—and *their* Father. It was something He spoke with great joy, after the circle of golden communion between the Triune God was fully restored—

"Do not hold on to me, for I have not yet ascended to the Father. Go instead to my brothers and tell them, 'I am ascending to my Father and your Father, to my God and your God'" (John 20:17).

When He said it, He was radiating with the strong bright white light of holiness that raised Him from the dead. It was a light that the Father had sent in full strength to restore His Son. But despite the terrifying power of the light of holiness, the women did not feel any fear because they were drawn close by *love*. It was something they were now meant to share with everyone—

"Jesus told us to tell you that God is *your* Father too."

It was a truth they would need to advance the apostolic gospel in the earth. For they could not access their full inheritance without this revelation of what Christ had achieved on our behalf—a revelation that we too are now full-blooded sons and daughters. And yet, no one could convince Thomas.

It was a week later and doors were firmly locked because everyone was afraid that the Jews would kill them in the same way they killed Jesus. Thomas stood resolute, determined that everything he was told was cooked up by the apostles. He boasted to them,

"Unless I see the nail marks in his hands and put my finger where the nails were, and put my hand into his side, I will not believe" (John 20:24).

Now the flash of light came again, but this time it was accompanied by a sonic boom as well, which erupted like a gunshot in the middle of the room. For the atmosphere was thick with humidity that day and the rift in space-time sometimes had this effect. It was the same way that Daniel knew Gabriel had come to him **"in swift flight"**—it was like an inter-dimensional sonic boom.[31] Even though the apostles had seen him before and fully believed, they were terrified by the sound of his arrival. So, he stretched his hands towards them and said, **"Peace be with you!" (John 20:26)**

The Lord turned to Thomas and smiled. He gave instructions that proved He knew everything Thomas had said and thought in his heart—

"Put your finger here; see my hands. Reach out your hand and put it into my side. Stop doubting and believe."

The Lord said it in a way that imparted both holy fear and perfect love and Thomas obeyed immediately. As he put his hands on the real flesh of the Lord's nail-scarred hands, tears began to stream down both his face and the Lord's. For

---

[31] See Daniel 9:21.

the circle of golden light now flowed between the two of them, just as it had flowed between the Father and the Son. Thomas looked at the face of the Lord and said with holy awe, **"My Lord and my God!"**

As soon as he said it, one more blood-red horse stepped into the room, this one dressed for war and destined to head east to lay gospel tracks from Jerusalem to Baghdad to India. It was a horse that would have to press through unbelief every step of the way as Thomas preached the apostolic gospel and planted churches in places where no foundation had ever been laid before. The Lord looked over at the red horse and knew that Thomas' discovery was a parable for the great faith that would be imparted to the churches he would plant in the far east. He now turned to him and prophesied —

"Because you have seen me, you have believed; blessed are those who have not seen and yet have believed" (John 20:29).

It was something they would do in Baghdad and India when Thomas evangelized them—they would believe without seeing. But it was also something they would do millennia in the future, as all of Asia came to the Lord. They would believe without seeing and be more blessed than any of those in the room.

7 | Ascending the Mountain of God

It happened on the anniversary of the day when Moses ascended the mountain and met with God face to face. It happened on the same day that Moses first saw the Father's glory and heard Him declare His own name and eternal nature as Moses himself recorded—

Then the Lord came down in the cloud and stood there with him and proclaimed his name, the Lord.

And he passed in front of Moses, proclaiming, "The Lord, the Lord, the compassionate and gracious God, slow to anger, abounding in love and faithfulness,

maintaining love to thousands, and forgiving wickedness, rebellion and sin. Yet he does not leave the guilty unpunished; he punishes the children and their children for the sin of the parents to the third and fourth generation (Exodus 34:5-7)

It was on this day, 1500 years earlier that Moses laid hold of the golden circle of fellowship between Father and Son and stood right in the middle of it. Moses drank in the glory and the love of the Father so fully that he descended from the mountain shining with the full radiance of that golden light.[32] But the people were terrified and begged him

---

[32] See Exodus 34:29.

to cover his face.[33] They wanted no part of the golden circle simply because they either refused or were unable to *understand it.* It was why Israel could not and would not recognize or acknowledge their Messiah. It was why they were blinded to the true nature of their heavenly Father. It was why they wandered in the wilderness and begged for *earthly* flesh instead of the nourishing meat of knowing Him. Yet, even in Israel's many rebellions, the Father's love and wisdom proceeded with His plan to unveil and reveal His full purposes, to draw them in again to His full glory, and ultimately restore them into the golden circle of fellowship.

And now 1500 years later, the descendants of those who said "no" to the golden light of fellowship now waited with anticipation to receive it. They waited with expectation in Zion, just as Moses had once waited on Sinai.

Moses' journey to Sinai was a journey of revelation. He had met the Father at the burning bush. He had seen great signs and wonders in carrying out Israel's deliverance from Egypt. He had heard the Father's voice as He lamented the suffering of the Father's children and received wisdom to call for their deliverance. But now, these waiting here had seen something even greater. They had not seen the Red Sea part, but they had seen countless demonized people restored to their right mind. They had seen the dead raised, the lepers cleansed, the sick healed. They had heard the words of wisdom the Son spoke and seen him multiply their lunch. But most importantly, they understood that through His sacrifice, He had purchased the right to remove the veil of

---

[33] See Exodus 34:30.

separation from all of humanity. They understood the theological basis by which they could now ascend to lay hold of a deeper communion with the Father. And the Father knew it too and waited for the day circled on his calendar to release the full weight of restoration.

But the last few weeks had taken a toll on them. Some allowed doubt to sneak into their minds and they left the upper room. Others were afraid of persecution and had little ones at home so they *had* to leave for their sake. Many left because they were offended that the Lord appeared to the twelve and not to them—so they began to question their accounts of everything that had happened. Others reasoned they could meet with the Father at home just as well as they could meet with Him *here*—so why bother?

Having seen the golden light that shone from the Son of God when He spoke about the Father, the hunger *increased* in those that remained. When their numbers dwindled down to 150, they began to tell themselves, "I don't care if I'm the only one left. I'm not leaving. He said to wait and I will obey." Some of them were assaulted by the fiercest doubts and fears as the powers of darkness tried to rob them of their inheritance. Even though the Spirit had not yet come in power, they had to sift through every thought, determining what was holy, what was completely natural and wholesome, and what was *profane*. In those days, they developed a quality of discernment that served as a foundation for the rest of their lives. And so, as they were waiting, their thoughts and emotions were refined. As some of the people left, their toxic thoughts and emotions departed with them. When a fierce gossiper left, the temptation to gossip about the apostles left with him. When a busy-body who found fault with everything that happened in the small community left, the temptation to accuse other people without good cause left with her. I was reminded of what Malachi prophesied and wondered if it was about this group—

This third I will put into the fire;
  I will refine them like silver
  and test them like gold.
They will call on my name
  and I will answer them;
I will say, 'They are my people,'
  and they will say, 'The Lord is our God'" (Zechariah 13:9).

Those who remained developed a kind of hive-mindset. For as the apostles began to declare the same scriptures the Lord had declared, the golden light began to sweep over them in waves. Revelation came gently, as an inner witness. And each fresh revelation stirred up more hunger and faith. And greater faith caused them to pray with more fervency and profound power. John got up and begin reading his notes from one of Christ's private messages to the twelve—it was the first time that most of them had heard it:

"My prayer is not for them alone. I pray also for those who will believe in me through their message,
  "that all of them may be one, Father, just as you are in me and I am in you. May they also be in us so that the world may believe that you have sent me.

"I have given them the glory that you gave me, that they may be one as we are one—

"I in them and you in me—so that they may be brought to complete unity. Then the world will know that you sent me and have loved them even as you have loved me.

"Father, I want those you have given me to be with me where I am, and to see my glory, the glory you have given me because you loved me before the creation of the world.

"Righteous Father, though the world does not know you, I know you, and they know that you have sent me.

"I have made you known to them, and will continue to make you known in order that the love you have for me may be in them and that I myself may be in them" (John 17:20-26).

The realization hit them with great power—He had personally prayed for *them.* He had said that the same glory, the same fellowship He enjoyed with the Father from "before the creation of the world" was now available to *them.* Moses was a prophet and invited everyone to be prophets. Many prophets followed in his train. But now, the Son of God was inviting all of them to be sons and daughters of God and follow in *His* train. *They* could see the same glory, know the same love, access the same limitless wells of wisdom and revelation and power that the Son of God had access to.

But there was another promise here too—the circle wasn't just between them and the Father. It was between themselves and *each other*. An unbroken golden circle that encompassed everyone. When that circle was properly established, they knew nothing could shake it.

The fulfillment came at nine o'clock in the morning. A sound like a freight train, a sound of rushing wind filled the whole house. It was the same sound that filled the garden and caused Adam and Eve to run after they had sinned. But now it was being restored. The Father was returning again to walk with His children in the garden of delights and enjoy sweet fellowship with them. It was a walk just like the walk of the Son, a walk that restored their memory of who they were and who they were destined to be. It was a walk that restored their memory of their Father's great love and grace. As the Father revealed Himself to each one with a unique revelation that each one needed to encounter, the full weight of the encounter began to burn from within each face. Unholy thoughts and feelings fled from their hearts and minds as birds scatter from a gunshot. They reeled like drunk people under the weight of perfect love and the thrill of pent-up wisdom and revelation in the Father's heart that He now imparted to them without limit.

Just as He had raised His horse up by pouring into it a stream of restorative light, life, and love, He now poured the full lightning strength of His presence and power into those gathered there. And so it was that 1500 years after the law of love was written only on stone, it was now written on 120 *hearts and minds*. What could not be accomplished with laws written on stone could now be accomplished with love written on hearts by the Spirit of God.[34]

Just as Moses ascended the mountain and met with the Father before he came back down to meet with the people, the 120 lingered in the presence of His spirit until they received the full impartation the Father had reserved for them. They ascended and encountered him in spiritual Zion. Although most did not see the angels and the blood-red horses, they were surrounded by them as the Father imparted to them messages and works of power to carry throughout the earth. And so, they descended from Zion riding the blood-red horses. They prophesied the message they had been given about the Son of God and everyone heard it in their own language. And on the anniversary of the day that the people begged Moses to cover His face, 3000 turned their faces back to the Father and learned to walk with Him in restored fellowship much greater than Moses.[35]

The riders of the blood-red horses were now filled with the same fire as the horses. They too now longed to go throughout the earth. And so now horses and riders became one and thus began the gallop of the blood-red horses throughout the earth. Yet even this was merely preparing the way for the greater levels of restoration yet to come.

---

[34] See Ezekiel 36:25-27.

[35] See 2 Corinthians 3:7-18 for the full description of this theology.

"The next stable was filled with creatures with heads like lions... They were clothed in a powerful armor that twinkled with flashes of lightning, all of which made them impervious to darkness."

8 | The Last White War-Horses

I stood again next to the stable of white war-horses. The wooden stall was now decorated with countless ribbons of different colors and sizes. Some of the war-horses and trainers wore beautiful crowns to testify of all they had released and established in the earth. There seemed to be many more white war-horses than before, but all of them now had crowns except for 70, who remained now in the center of the pasture. Hundreds of other horses who had completed their race and thousands of trainers now gathered around them and they were all *whispering.* I looked at the plaque again which said—

EVERY HORSE AND TRAINER MUST BE
TRAINED TO HEAR MY WHISPER.

The same trainer who had spoken to me before now returned, although he was walking at a much slower pace because he was no longer in a hurry. He seemed to take forever to arrive. When he finally reached me, he leaned in close and whispered—

"These are the last white war horses and they will face the greatest battles as they bring spiritual awakening, revival, restoration, and reformation to every nation on earth. They will not succeed unless they also learn from every horse and trainer that came before. This is why the cloud of witnesses is opening up much more for your generation than any that came before. You must listen to the wisdom from the past they carry."

I realized that the reason revival was taking so long to come to my own generation is because far more training required than anyone anticipated. And no one here seemed to be in a hurry because they were more concerned with the *quality* of transmission of each message of wisdom than the *speed* of its transmission. After a long time of hushed silence, when it was clear that all of the decorated horses and trainers had finished their whispers, the Father's horse left its stall. It shone now as radiant as lightning and the Lord himself was riding on it. Horse and rider drew near to the 70 war horses and the Lord leaned in close to breathe on each one of them. He now stood facing them as the grand marshal of the whole grand assembly and declared over them the same words the Father said long ago—

"Holiness has given you the power of an indestructible life!"

The first time He said it, the 70 white war-horses received an abiding whisper so that they could now *know* the Father's perfect will no matter what was unfolding on the earth. They were now equipped to hear from the Lord about every matter—from the smallest details of their personal lives to the weightiest decisions that would impact many lives. And they could discern the holy thoughts of God from their natural human thoughts. They could immediately recognize the shadow of darkness and banish the thoughts that proceeded from its influence. And then the Lord spoke again—

"Holiness has given you the power of an indestructible life!"

This time, the seventy white war horses were given the power to *obey* every whisper they heard. And through obedience, their discernment came as sharp as a knife. For obedience honed their skills to the point that they would know about everything before it happened and take steps to prepare. Nothing could catch them unaware anymore.

The Lord stepped off the Father's horse and went to them in His resplendent garments as high priest. It reminded me of when he had stepped off the horse and approached the Most Holy Place the first time to bless all of mankind. He repeated the words once again now—

"Holiness has given you the power of an indestructible life!"

When he said it, the 70 were instantly filled with the same measure of the Father's glory that the Son carried. When he said it, they found themselves pulled into the same circle of fellowship. And yet, they went far beyond the golden light to find a light as bright as lightning that could pierce through any darkness. Through impartation directly from the Son, they had now learned to hear the Father's whisper, obey, and move in power in the same manner He had. The thunder now shook the whole assembly as the Spirit of Holiness now spoke over them, "Go throughout the earth!" They vanished in a flash of pure white light and with a great rumbling of thunder.

After they vanished, I walked back to the rear of the stall. All of the trainers were now gathered to watch it, much in the same way that people gather around a television whenever major events are unfolding. One after another, the ribbons and trophies and awards the war horses were gaining as they went throughout the earth appeared. However, I noticed that every time some new award appeared, new crowns also appeared on various horses and trainers identifying those who had finished their race. It was because they shared in the reward of everything they sowed into—this was true whether they helped to train the war horses directly or because their lingering influence from centuries ago had simply helped to prepare the way. The greatest awards were made of pure silver, which sparkled with the light of heaven. I saw a massive silver platter recognizing a move of God that swept through all of Asia and had such a massive impact on the earth that it made great inroads into the Middle East, Russia, and Eastern Europe.

There was a particular post where the ribbons from Europe and North America were beginning to appear. The post was named "The Pillar of Trans-Atlantic Revivalism" and it was closely watched by the Wesley brothers, George Whitefield, Charles Finney, Evan Roberts, William Seymour, and many others. The reports of awakening in North America and Western Europe were stacked up like Jenga[36]

---

[36] *Jenga* is a popular game in which wooden blocks are moved and stacked to create the tallest tower possible.

blocks, with the oldest awakenings at the bottom and the most recent ones on top. In this manner, it was clear to everyone watching that what was unfolding now would not have been possible were it not for every "block" that had come before. However, there was also a great warning in this —for if the old foundations were moved, the whole tower would come tumbling down and it would have to be built up all over again. I could not see the other regions of the world in this manner—perhaps I saw only the regions I have sowed the most prayer into.

9 | The Father's Horse Re-Visited

Despite the great victories of the red horses and the white war horses, there was still a great weight hanging upon the Father's heart. He heard the same desperate cry He heard from His own horse, but now it was erupting from the earth below with a volume and intensity that the whole world could hear. The words came in desperate painful cries, once again like the voice of a child in great danger that pulls on the emotions and demands immediate intervention—

"Help me, Father!"

"Why, Father, why?"

The sounds were erupting from a generation that faced *the same* powers of darkness that crucified the Lord. For they too had been beaten, bruised, mocked, and martyred. They now faced the same piercing spiritual darkness that the Lord faced when He was on the cross. The darkness was wrapped around them like slimy black cords and it prevented them from seeing Him, just as the Son could not see His Father when on the cross. The dark cords were like tethers that kept them earth-bound, blind, and miserable. But when the Father looked down upon these millions of desperate cries, He could trace no journeys they had taken with Him in the past as He could for His most-loved Son. When he looked down on them and saw their suffering, there was no memory of *past communion*, no golden circle of light in the ancient mists of history to draw from. And so, the Father looked decisively *into the future*.

He looked and saw, as a single image, these multitudes riding with Him through all the long stretches of eternity. He saw them share in the joy of His glory. He saw them living forever in His house, their days stretched long and filled with His great pleasure. He looked forward and saw an unbroken circle of love that flowed between the Triune God and these multitudes as they rode throughout the cosmos and beyond. And so in the same way His Son experienced revelation from the future as a memory and felt the warmth, now the Father's eyes flooded with tears of love. He would not rescue them because of anything they had accomplished in the past—He would rescue them on the basis of what Christ accomplished and because of who they would become *in the future*.

And so, now *the Father* descended from heaven to walk upon the earth. It wasn't the first time. He had given Moses a glimpse of Himself and remained His close friend, eventually speaking to him **"face to face."**[37] But Moses' generation wanted no part of it. They begged Moses, **"Speak to us yourself and we will listen. But do not have God speak to us or we will die" (Exodus 20:19).** It was a foolish generation that was offered the full light of the face of the Father, and yet chose to remain in the outer darkness,

---

[37] See Exodus 33:11.

left with only the hollow shell of His household rules—rules designed for servants and workers, not the sons and daughters who would know the true intentions of His heart. But while that generation was given light freely and chose darkness, this generation longed for the light of His face and yet remained bound as the swirling storms of darkness reached their full maturity in the earth and became binding cords on their hearts and minds.

When the Father descended, the storms of darkness were torn asunder as by a great lightning sword. When His feet touched the earth, the cords were shattered. He would rescue them because they would love Him *in the future.* It was a perfect fulfillment of David's prophetic words in Psalm 18, but now for an entire generation bound by darkness instead of one man:

I called to the Lord, who is worthy of praise, and I have been saved from my enemies.
The cords of death entangled me; the torrents of destruction overwhelmed me.
The cords of the grave coiled around me; the snares of death confronted me.

In my distress I called to the Lord; I cried to my God for help. From his temple, he heard my voice; my cry came before him, into his ears.
The earth trembled and quaked, and the foundations of the mountains shook; they trembled because he was angry.
Smoke rose from his nostrils; consuming fire came from his mouth, burning coals blazed out of it.

He parted the heavens and came down; dark clouds were under his feet.

He mounted the cherubim and flew; he soared on the wings of the wind.

He made darkness his covering, his canopy around him—the dark rain clouds of the sky.

Out of the brightness of his presence clouds advanced, with hailstones and bolts of lightning.

The Lord thundered from heaven; the voice of the Most High resounded.

He shot his arrows and scattered the enemy, with great bolts of lightning he routed them.

The valleys of the sea were exposed and the foundations of the earth laid bare at your rebuke, Lord, at the blast of breath from your nostrils.

He reached down from on high and took hold of me; he drew me out of deep waters.

He rescued me from my powerful enemy, from my foes, who were too strong for me.

They confronted me in the day of my disaster, but the Lord was my support.

He brought me out into a spacious place; he rescued me because he delighted in me (Psalm 18:3-19).

When the Father revealed Himself, a measure of power was released far beyond what any number of intercessors, prophets, and worshippers could release. For the Father's revelation was not in any way limited by how much intercession, worship, or prophetic declaration was released by others. For the door was too heavy to open, the darkness to strong. So now, *He* opened the door and stepped through on His own. He was now moving *sovereignly,* and in his perfect justice unleashed the full strength of His wrath upon the powers of darkness. It was an anger and jealousy for His children born of pure love.

Now, the Father cradled an entire generation in his arms and wept over them with the same measure of love He reserved for His one and only Son. It was an intercession beyond intercession and it was the only intervention powerful enough to release the children of God *from the future* from the cords of darkness *in the now.*

The Father's Horse

10 | When the Father Shows Up

The grasses were trampled from the traffic of hundreds of thousands, but the open field did not have any trash in it. It had all begun in someone's backyard. A simple night of worship. A few guitars. Someone shared a few scriptures. They did not see it, but they felt it when the Father came into the meeting to deliver them from the cords of darkness. Although they could not see His eyes, they could feel the piercing gaze of His love as He spoke into them,

"Holiness has given you the power of an indestructible life!"

A time of long silence followed. Then weeping. Then tears of joyful love. Everyone in the meeting was brought into the golden circle of fellowship with the Father. Now, the golden circle revealed itself as a weapon of great power. For, like a razor-sharp buzz saw, it cut the greasy cords of darkness asunder. Jealousy, self-hatred, temptation, and doubt were fully revealed and banished from every heart and mind by the penetrating light. In their place, the Father now poured into each of them the full strength of His love, His power, and His seven-fold Spirit. He imparted a deep level of Wisdom beyond what any had known before. In the silence, the teachers among them saw everything they would need to say now and in the future. The shepherds saw every wound they must heal and who they must gather now and in the future. The evangelists were given boldness and the power to work great signs both now and in the future. People had their theology all wrong because they believed Moses' generation—they wanted an intermediary to speak to the Father for them. But that's never what the Father wanted and now He made them *all* prophets as He downloaded blueprints to restore His children in the earth.

It continued for seven hours—weeping, laughing, crying, prophetic songs, prayers. They didn't notice at first, but the stars did not wheel across the sky as they encountered the Father. The sun was not making its way towards the horizon. But there was a time when the Father finished His business with them. It was after every dark cord was severed and they had received everything He desired to impart. It was the first time they looked at their watches—and only 20 minutes had passed. I think the Father did it to show that it really was *Him* who showed up that night. They looked at each other and marveled, *"We encountered our Father tonight!"*

It also happened when Stephen was driving twenty years ago. For a long time, He had been drawing nearer and nearer to the Father. He kept seeing it—He was *in the Father*—and the Father was *in Him*. But it was more than a mere visualization. It was real. When the Father's love was poured out, he found himself revisiting his whole life—past, present, and future. His soul became whole and he learned his destiny well. He saw the generation he was called to raise up. He was slowly being squeezed between the glorious weight of the Father *in* Him and the Father *around* Him until he felt like a thin narrow wafer about to break to feed his generation. The weight of the Father's glory was crushing his soul. But he still wanted much more of it, for the communion and passion he was gaining were of far greater weight than the things he was losing. And the more time He spent with the Father, the purer his love became for the *Son,* and for his own generation. When Stephen's body was broken in the accident, hearts broke with Him. But when his body was buried in the ground, the crumbs from the thin wafer Stephen had become were sprinkled like golden seeds all across the East Coast and sown deeply into the land. It went back to what Jesus said—

"The hour has come for the Son of Man to be glorified.

"Very truly I tell you, unless a kernel of wheat falls to the ground and dies, it remains only a single seed. But if it dies, it produces many seeds.

"Anyone who loves their life will lose it, while anyone who hates their life in this world will keep it for eternal life.

"Whoever serves me must follow me; and where I am, my servant also will be. My Father will honor the one who serves me" (John 12:23-26).

It was not merely a declaration of the atonement that only Christ could purchase with His blood. It was also a declaration about the power of martyrdom. For those who followed Christ in death, also follow him in glorification. Just as Christ ascended and gave gifts, everyone who followed showered their gifts down too. For having reached the full measure of sonship, the Father looks at the death of every martyr with the same depth of love He felt for His Son on the cross and He *responds* with the full strength of His power. Just as Christ multiplied Himself through His death, so would all who die with him multiply themselves. And now there were 1,000 Stephens along the East Coast, leaders of youth revivals who *abided* in the Father's glory all the time and were pleased to be squeezed thin in the middle.

Now, I looked out on the sea of faces here. 200,000 youth in an open field. It was the glory that brought them in. It was the glory that kept them here, singing and weeping all night, as fresh revelations from the Father were poured into them in full strength. Although some of songs that opened heaven were written in the secret place of their garages and backyards, many of the songs came spontaneously, as they erupted from their communion with the Father. And because the songs *came* from heaven, they had the power to *open* heaven. I was amazed that they carried such a maturity of love, being so young. And that was before the preachers got up to share.

The first was a young man in his twenties. He had the power to look right into heaven the whole time He was speaking, so that *every word* came straight from the throne. He carried a depth of wisdom that could not be unraveled with any human philosophies or arguments because Wisdom led him to preach a clear and uncompromised apostolic gospel, with His primary message being, *"We are finishing what Christ started and we can't be stopped!"* Although the

They looked at each other and marveled,
"We encountered our Father tonight!"

crowd roared as he made his points, many people were seen scattered throughout the crowd, or on trampled lawns, or strewn out on blankets, each of them weeping in their own first-time encounters with the Father's glory.

It was not unusual in these times to see the Father's glory emanating from people's faces. And being young and teachable, many quickly learned to recognize exactly what aspect of the Father someone was encountering when this soft light began to shine from their skin—for they had encountered the same thing. Words became less necessary between believers as the golden circle of the Father's glory began to draw them all together as one. From time to time, someone would get up to share their gift. A 17-year-old girl named Elizabeth, who carried the mantle of Maria Woodworth Etter, got up to share almost every night. She had raised several people from the dead and there were always many people healed and delivered when she spoke, but that's not why they feared her. It was the frozen man that gave them all the fear of God when she ascended to the stage. He was a heckler and when she was drawing from the full strength of the Father's wisdom and glory and power, he began to decry her as a fraud. The next day, he was still standing there, his finger pointed towards her, frozen in the Father's glory. She wasn't heckled again after that.

It was here, as they sang all through the night, that the Father rent the heavens and came down to walk among them and cut the cords of death from a generation. Although no one in the small group where it began had the eyes to see Him, there were many in this assembly now who were beginning to walk in the powers of the age to come. The neglected seeds of gifts and callings rejected by every generation before them were now poured into their laps as a blessing too large to contain.   And so it was that this generation, now rescued by the Father, was given the work of finishing what the Lord started.

Many of the youth were not only receiving their own gifts and callings, but were also filled with every blessing the Father had intended for their bloodline in all of history, but which darkness had held back.   Now that the dark cords were cut and the communion was restored, there was no limit on the gifts.   And so, the gifts were greatly multiplied and the supernatural signs that followed them were beyond comprehension.

11 | A Seat for the Son

In the vast open landscape where multitudes gathered in the Father's glory each night, as new gifts and callings were resurfacing, some from a long slumber in the past, the Living Christ showed up to walk among them. He held up a golden stirrup, which was the only piece left when He divided up his saddle. It was something He had saved for this generation—a foot hold. For He had imparted to them a revelation of His Father's glory that would allow them to dig their feet in deep and go higher. He wanted them to ascend with Him for a season. But now, they must finish the work He started. Now, it was time to *descend*.

As the living Christ held the golden stirrup up in the air, the young apostle continued to preach his greatest message — *"We are finishing what Christ started and we can't be stopped! We don't fear death anymore, because it has no sting any longer. We don't fear sickness and disease. We don't fear any shadow of heart and mind, for we are seated with Christ and beholding the Father's Glory."* It was not a message that declared what he hoped would happen—it was an acknowledgment of what was already true for this great assembly of youth. As he spoke, a great whirlwind began to swirl around them, for the living Christ stood in the center of the assembly, holding the golden stirrup high in the air. They had been faithful with it and had gone higher for many weeks and now it was time to give them much more.

As the whirlwind rose, several small pieces of the saddle were blown in by the winds and reattached to the stirrup, complete with the meticulous golden stitching, so that a strip of pure white leather was now hanging from the stirrup. Soon, the whole saddle began to take shape, although it looked much more glorious than before it was divided, because now it was *multiplied* in its size, light, and power. For the saddle did not only carry the Father's memories of his long walks with His one and only Son. But now the saddle also carried the Father's memories of his long walks with a great multitude beyond calculation. And now all of the gifts, callings, and mantles carried faithfully by everyone in this multitude were carefully and powerfully fashioned together. It was like what happened in the upper room, except that the whirlwind did not merely pull in the glory from the present. It also had the power to pull in all of the glory from those who came before. The full expression of the priestly ephod was now pulled in to the saddle from its place above all of time and eternity. The full expression of king and prophet. The full expression of shepherd and teacher. And as these were restored back to the proper headship of Christ and re-unified under His authority, they grew to a strength, size, and magnitude of brightness that far exceeded what had come when the Father's horse descended into hell for the first time. It was the difference between one star—the Morning Star—which served to put the darkness on notice that the dawn was coming and the full expression of dawn. It was like all the galaxies of stars swirling together to form a blazing sun of incalculable gravity.

When the saddle was complete, the Lord held it out in thin air, as if waiting for the Father's horse to come. However, something even more strange happened. The youth were swept into it first. They became the legs. Then every other generation, older generations still living and those who came before, became the torso, eyes, ears, nose, and mouth. The assembly of the saints was now united to become a *seat* for the Son because it was time for the Son to descend a second time and finish his work in partnership with them.

The Father's horse now stood tall, glorious, and unshakeable. It was much taller and far more powerful than it had ever been before. For now, all of the love the Father had for every child of God was woven into the fiber of its being. Its muscles rippled with anticipation. Although its body sparkled like pure crystal filled with ripping lightning, its hair flashed different colors in the whirlwind, for it was manifesting all of the different natures of God that had been revealed to everyone who had become part of it. The Father's horse had finally become a full and complete revelation of the Father's glory. Likewise, when Christ took up His sword again, it seemed to have far more power than before. While it is true that He had purchased all and longed to complete His work in hell—the time for completion had not yet come because the harvest was not mature. Key pieces had been missing. But now, it was time.

The Son now put his foot in the golden stirrup and swung up high to find his place upon the high seat of the Father's horse. He was now seated upon a people already unified, their many and varied gifts and callings fitted as restored puzzle pieces that fit together perfectly. But it was He who completed them. And horse and rider became one when He sat. For the golden circle of unbroken fellowship now rose to a new level of power. The Son wanted to descend and vanquish hell immediately, so great was the strength—He knew He could do it. But the Father whispered to the Son—and to the horse—to come up higher for another drink of Wisdom before beginning the final conquest of the powers of darkness.

A great portal of fire opened up and the horse dove into it. Now the horse ascended like a rocket and galloped all through the long stretches of time and eternity, through distant galaxies. As it rode, the dying nebulae and clouds of dark gas were restored by the thunder of his hooves. What had been dead now came alive, and multitudes of new stars were born. It passed terrible lightnings on the outer reaches as it dove far beyond the material universe and began its ascent through all the heavens—those belonging to the natural world, those of a spiritual nature, and those that defy categorization. Now the ascent reached dizzying heights and the horse began to *grow* in size all the more, as the people, their callings, and their height and depth of fellowship with Father, Son, and Spirit expanded their *capacity* for love, power, and glory. As the horse grew in size, I remembered that Solomon wasn't just given great depth of wisdom, but also the capacity of his heart was expanded to be as **"measureless as the sand on the sea shore."** This empowered Him to hold *more* of God's thoughts about us, which scripture tells us **"outnumber the grains of sand"** (see 1 Kings 4:29, Psalm 139:17-18)

They now galloped far beyond the stable of the Father's horse. They now re-traced every stone of fire where the Son and Father had enjoyed private fellowship, for the Son could not reveal to all of those *in Him* the full weight of the golden circle. And they kept galloping, through mountains made of solid gold and silver and lead. They kept galloping, through strange and varied landscapes smoking with fragrant incense that caused the nostrils of the Father's horse to flare with fire and its eyes to burn with revelations of eternity that made all of heaven and earth look incredibly small in comparison. It galloped through long stretches of pure white light, bursting through planes of sparkling crystal that rippled with lightning. It was all only the *beginning* of the where the Father knew they would go together. In the whole journey, I felt like we were re-treading the ground Christ covered when He **"passed through the heavens"**—that's heavens plural—as high priest on our behalf, only now we were allowed to go *with* Him for we had now become a mature priesthood by allowing Him to rest upon us and direct our every step (See Hebrews 4:14).

Now, the two brown and white mustangs and their riders joined to the right and left. Having eaten all the revelation that had been given about themselves and about this generation, the riders' white hair and beards glowed with the joy and fire they carried. It was when these mustangs came alongside that the assembly in the Father's horse truly understood the Father's size, which so fully dwarfed the cosmos—and all the pain of the past—that they were inebriated with a confidence to overcome all things. I realized they had overcome great battles in their times because they had come to personally know the greatness of their God. I wondered how big we'd have to perceive the Father as in order to win the final battle.

The mustangs knew the way to the Father's house and they now came as an escort, to further train and impart to the Father's horse a deeper mystery it did not yet know—they traced ancient paths of fellowship so narrow they seemed to squeeze everyone that passed through. These were like gates that were both terrible and delightful to cross because they fiercely dealt with any remaining selfishness, yet also imparted the selfless love and holiness of God. The journey of the Father's horse through the heavens felt like a thousand deaths, for as each level of the journey was finished it was dwarfed by what came next. All of the senses were shaken by the transitions between the levels until the Father's horse finally reached a place of green pasture and rest.

When they first began treading on the green grass before they reached the Father's house, there was a small worm eating a single blade. And yet because of the colossal size of the Father, everything in this realm was infinitely *bigger* than anything in the earth or in any of the other realms they had passed through. And this little worm, eating a single blade of grass on the Father's lawn, was large enough to hold the entire cosmos in its belly. The multitude had now grown in their approach, so that their own stature reached the immensity of the Father's stature—but most were unaware of it unless they *looked back*. I remembered that man was made in *His* image, but this immensity of scale was one aspect of His nature I was surprised to see embodied by His children. I thought of the apostle Peter's words—

His divine power has given to us all things that pertain to life and godliness, through the knowledge of Him who called us by glory and virtue,

by which have been given to us exceedingly great and precious promises, that through these you may be partakers of the divine nature, having escaped the corruption that is in the world through lust (2 Peter 1:3-4, NKJV)

The journey had "given to us all things"—keys for living life in His presence, keys for infusing every stop with more and more Godliness, keys for overcoming in dark times. And these keys had all been imparted to us through revelation from the Father and the Son. And the primary key was that we were yoked together with Christ, fully submitted to His headship. This was vitally important because it allowed us to tap into the divine nature that belonged to Him alone. But by being united with *Christ,* we could drink it in and experience the same love, power, and joy of the Father that he felt. The knowledge we gained was not the kind that puffs up, but rather the deep spiritual knowledge that brought greater humility and fear of the Lord than we had before, along with a willingness to serve one another in selfless love.[38] There was never a risk of seeing ourselves as "too big" because no matter how big we

---

[38] See Philippians 2:1-11.

became, a deeper revelation of the Father's immensity stood before us like an open door to a higher and deeper realm of the Father's glory.

It was strange to see the vast landscape surrounding the Father's house—the landscape of heaven—and find it felt so much like earth, but like the Father, it appeared glorified, perfected, and expanded in size. The sky there was constantly changing as the clouds refracted rays of silver, gold, turquoise, and bright flames of fire in radiant colors. The clouds reflected what the Father was thinking about. As I gazed at them, I realized the Father's horse had also stopped, and everyone else was mesmerized by the unfolding scene above. At first, the clouds began to appear like the heads of birds—sweet sparrows and song birds.[39] And as these appeared, it was like an explosion of stars and many lights descended and gathered around us. They were the angels who worship the face of the Father, continually singing new songs to magnify the light of His face. And now they were joining us in our ride, no matter where we would ascend—or descend—to. Next, the heads appearing in the clouds appeared like great birds of prey—raptors of terrifying scale and size and ferocity. I saw eagles and falcons and the owls who keep the watch at night. And as these appeared, many flames of fire descended around us with a great wind and I knew that these angelic heralds would remain with us too.

---

[39] Much of this paragraph is based on prophetic dreams my grandfather had in 1979, which he wrote down and kept hidden to preserve for a future generation.

I continued watching until a vast gate opened up in the sky, crowned on every side with the heads of white lions. The Father said, *"It is time for the lion gate to open!"* and now there descended around us many creatures who did not look like angels at all, but more like the locusts Joel describes or the living creatures John and Ezekiel describe. They were incredibly strange, but they reflected a depth of wisdom, love, and power that showed they were probably more firmly planted in the golden circle of fellowship than any of the angels who had come before. These angels emerged with great terror, to remove all that was unholy, to bring judgement, and to pave the way for the great restoration soon to unfold. They came from the eternal realms, from levels much higher than I could see, but their destination was *earth* and I knew they too would join us as escorts when we descended.

As I continued to look up, I saw a vast tent, of much greater scale than the whole cosmos. I was reminded of Psalm 104,

The Lord wraps himself in light as with a garment; he stretches out the heavens like a tent
and lays the beams of his upper chambers on their waters. He makes the clouds his chariot and rides on the wings of the wind.
He makes winds his messengers, flames of fire his servants" (Psalm 104:2-4)

When the Son stepped into the tent with the Father, He vanished for a long time, but I could see in my mind's eye that they were gathered around a great table with many maps and blueprints spread out. I knew that the Father was now revealing to the Son every strategy He would need to win the final battle. He was unveiling most—but not all—of the blueprints for building the City of God and fully restoring heaven and earth. There were some things the Father still wanted to keep as a surprise for His wedding day. As they remained there, the tent shone with a snowy white brilliance. It flashed like lightning as their conversation ebbed and flowed. The circle of golden fellowship now took on this greater brightness as new levels of wisdom and revelation were imparted to the Son, far greater than what had been revealed before.

The last thing I saw overwhelmed me and defied comprehension. The Father stooped down low and washed the feet of His most-loved Son. He wept with love as they remembered past, present, and future as one mind. But as He washed His feet, something new was in the water. There was a lightning-bright light of victory infused in the water, so that as the Father washed the Son's feet, He was shown levels of triumph He had never been shown before, and with them the strategies to bring each level into fullness of joy. He was shown how to *use* the authority He had in ways never before seen. As He washed His feet, the Son of God took on a radiance of terrible lightnings and I remembered that Jesus had said,

"But about that day or hour no one knows, not even the angels in heaven, nor the Son, but only the Father" (Matthew 24:36).

I remembered that there are some things the Father knows that He has not yet revealed to the Son. This was one of the times the Father freely poured out His deep knowledge upon the Son with such strength that He wept with joy, as though it was His first resurgent memory as a young child in Nazareth.

The Lord now stepped out of the Father's tent and brought the Father's washing basin to the grass. First, He invited only those who had answered His invitations in the past because He knew they would remain faithful in the future. The 70 white war horses stepped out first, emerging from the side of the Father's horse where they had remained united with the rest of the assembly. They bowed their heads low as their riders dismounted and approached the Lord. As the Lord washed their feet, they wept with Him for a long time. For the Son washed their feet with the same revelations the Father had given Him and these perfectly met the longing of the riders for greater depth. I feared those in the assembly of the Father's horse were missing out, but I looked back and saw the Father's horse eating the grass. As he ate, his eyes glowed with all the light of the heavens it had passed through as well as those which still lay beyond, for the grass itself carried a revelation of the eternal realms he would need as strength for the descent. After the riders were washed clean and all the dust of the world was purged from their heart and mind, there was no restriction at all on them anymore and the Lord pronounced over them,

"Holiness has given you the power of an indestructible life!"

When He said it, the same lightning that was in the Father's tent began to shine from their faces. He told them to reach down into the water of the basin and they each brought out battle maps and blueprints showing them how to bring victory to the earth by judging and removing the powers of darkness. It was a level of triumph they did not know was possible before the Lord showed them where to find it. I marveled that the Lord did not take long in passing along to those who were in close fellowship with him all that the Father had told Him.

They approached the white war horses now and washed them from head to foot with water from the basin. They also wept over their horses with all of the love of the Father and the Son, showering them with deep love, but also with a revelation of triumph that went far beyond anything seen before on the earth. As they did, it looked like the white horses got much stronger and shone an even brighter white. When they were done, they declared over their horses,

"Holiness has given you the power of an indestructible life!"

Having received their impartation, the riders re-mounted their horses and dove back into the Father's horse, where they were reunited with the rest of the assembly. When they did, the Father's horse shined with a pure light much more intense than ever before, as everyone included in its assembly had now received the revelation of love and power imparted from the Father and the Son. Now the Son mounted the horse, which shone as radiant as lightning, and shouted as a war-cry to drive the horse forward,

"Holiness has given you the power of an indestructible life!"

The Father's horse, after reaching dizzying heights and unfathomable expansions of size and scale in its journey, now felt a knot in its belly, like the moment where you reach the top of a roller coaster to begin the first great descent. The Father's horse took off at the speed of lightning, shrieking like a screaming eagle diving for its prey. As it departed, I noticed a tightly wrapped bundle tucked under the Lord's left arm that looked even more powerful than the lightning sword. I wondered what it was and reasoned it must be another kind of weapon because we were now bringing the final assault that would bind and banish from the earth all the powers of darkness.

The Father's Horse

12 | The Sun Stands Still

As the Father's horse was being reassembled with greater glory than before, something else was happening too. For the sons of darkness were coming to maturity and the gate was opened for the four horsemen to trample the earth in their full strength. The sickly horse was now vomiting in many places throughout the earth, releasing great plagues on crops, sicknesses that killed many babies, children, and elderly people, and poison in the atmosphere, land, and water. The counterfeit white horse was riding too as it sought to conquer every land, first by muttering dark incantations rooted in deception, and then with renewed threats of terror and violence. The red horse now had the power to stir up *new* hatreds instead of only relying on the ones that had been there a long time. Even family members turned on each other when he came to full strength. And the black horse heightened the weight and cruelty of everything else that was happening, for hungry people are much weaker and more prone to disease. Hungry people are also more prone to hatred when someone else is blamed and more easily deceived when the lie offers relief from their suffering. And so, in this way, the four horses grew in strength with each passing day and began to bring suffering on the earth that far exceeded the darkest moments in all of history.

When the four horses reached maturity, hell was convinced it had won and so it now poured out its full strength by unleashing a river of death on the earth from every gate of hell, positioned in many cities and regions around the globe, but mostly in the northern hemisphere. And now, as the Father's horse approached from afar, with a vanguard of witnesses and angelic hosts, the earth itself saw it coming and rejoiced. The army now drew closer armed with every conceivable spiritual weapon, but they had also taken on the *size* of the Father's house. So, when they saw the powers of darkness, those that Christ had left for them to take out, they did not say, **"We are only grasshoppers in their sight"** like the ten spies of Israel who brought back an evil report. Instead, knowing they now reflected the Father's immensity, they laughed like strong men ready for a fight, and shouted out to each other when they saw the powers of darkness and the sons of darkness and said, **"They will be bread for us!"** And so, an understanding of *scale* became an important foundation for keeping a mindset of victory for this final army. Yet, as they approached, the powers of darkness could not see them because they were still blinded by the pride of *their own* victory. Watching these powers of darkness was like watching a city that continues to bustle itself with activity until a great asteroid strikes to wipe it out.

The gates of hell were like vast portals in the earth that spewed out tar and then sucked it back in, pulling desperate souls into an inescapable darkness. But the tar also pulled in whole landscapes. There were sections of the earth where crops vanished, trees shriveled, and lack of fresh water reduced the Earth to dust wherever the powers of darkness were reaching their full maturity. It was like the earth was so possessed by evil that it was itself a beating heart of darkness, spewing the black tar out and sucking it back in, defiling the earth and the sons of men one moment and then swallowing them in its belly the next.

One of the two witnesses became so disgusted when he saw what was happening that he commanded the sun to stand still. As soon as he said it, one of the angels with a head of the lion went and stood in front of the sun. Immediately, the churning darkness ceased. The tar did not move, but everything that was being released from or swallowed by the gates of hell was forced to stop in its tracks. It was a strange thing, but time only stopped for the powers of darkness. While they were frozen and unmovable, the armies of heaven could accomplish their full purpose without hindrance. For they were the only army in the battle who could *transcend* time. It reminded me of when Joshua led the armies of God to kill the five kings of the Amorites. In a great battle that only foreshadowed this one, Joshua had already won the victory but he refused to see the enemies of God spared by the sword. He wanted *revenge*. And so, he spoke to the sun and moon,

"Sun, stand still over Gibeon; and Moon, in the Valley of Aijalon."
So the sun stood still, and the moon stopped, till the people had revenge upon their enemies" (Joshua 10:12-13).

It was a declaration the Father heard because it had originated from *Him* to begin with. Instantly, the flaming horses and chariots were released like lightnings. The horses with lion heads and their chariots of lightning riders with them, together with the angels of deep revelation from the golden chamber of the Father, all sped with great ferocity and precision to snatch the powers of darkness and defeat them. The attacking riders proclaimed the same words the horses did at the same time, so that it went out sounding as thunder.

I was surprised to see the chariots dive into the gates of hell themselves, to find the fallen watcher angels who had glorified themselves, defiled mankind, and destroyed the earth. The chariots of lightning returned in short order, as the powers of darkness were bound, gagged, and held with chains of impenetrable light. I thought I would see the powers of darkness shrieking with pain and terror from the light, but they lay as dead men, rendered unmovable by the suspension of time. I remembered they had been banished from the eternal realms. With lightning speed, the chariots now vanished into the heavens with a great thunder as they banished the powers of darkness to some other realm for an even weightier judgement in the future, a judgement where the fire that flows from the Father would tear them asunder, never to rise again. The chariots of lightning were a picture of the angels of God and holy people working in tandem to render binding judgements upon the powers of darkness— judgements so terrible and final they could no longer molest the earth. I looked a thousand years into the future and saw the faces of these powers of darkness melting off of them from the fire radiating from the faces of the saints. They could not stand or even approach the presence of the holiness that was yet to come in the future. But those who are wise will learn to bring this holiness into the *now,* that they might be untouchable by any power of darkness still remaining in this present age.

When the powers of darkness were removed from hell, I noticed something unimaginable—the bright light of holiness, the light of the golden circle of fellowship between Father and Son was now shining *from* the depths of the earth. It was a fire of consuming jealousy and love and began to suck all of the deep black tar back into hell and banish it from the earth. Spiritual darkness was stripped from the atmosphere, the earth, and the water. Winds now swept across the earth with gale force, sweeping every trace of lingering spiritual darkness from the earth. The angels represented by the falcons, eagles, and owls now joined the company of prophets and they uprooted anything still stained by spiritual darkness and threw it into the fire of jealousy now burning from every open portal. Not a single tree or rock was left untouched, but all defiled things were thrown in and consumed by the fire of jealous love.

I thought the sweet sparrows and songbirds would come first because they were the least significant, but they came last because they are the most important to the Father. A sound of singing began to erupt from all the earth, as the multitude of youth the Father had rescued from cords of darkness eagerly erupted with songs of heaven. The darkness that once held them was finally banished! As they sang, they sang from the depths of love that only one who is "forgiven much" can fully comprehend. The sound of their voices even changed the weather patterns, and new refreshing rains moved across the face of the earth. Rivers rose with pure clean water which washed away the radioactive dust on the landscape, revealing riverbeds that sparkled with precious jewels and gold dust. As they sang, the dry crooked trees once charred by war shook off their old branches and grew new ones. Buds, blossoms, and bright green leaves emerged to reflect the light of heaven. Song birds and honeybees returned. Then, the angel standing in front of the sun for the last and final battle re-joined the company, and time began anew. The hours were drawn out by the pleasure and joy released over what was unfolding, and time itself seemed much *longer* than ever before.

The Lord then unwrapped the package He had kept hidden under His left arm. It was the Father's tent, that which he had encountered on the furthest extent of His journey upon the Father's horse. As he unwrapped it, He remembered when the Father washed His feet there. He remembered the triumph He was shown. And he planted the golden stakes of the tent in every city and region that had faithfully prayed for Jerusalem before raising up the tent in its fullness on the earth. As the white tent rose like a canopy over Jerusalem, something strange happened. The heavens themselves were *rolled up* like a tent and now turned all of their light towards this place, as sunflowers turn their heads to gaze at the sun. This place was now becoming the center of the cosmos, the center of all time, the eternal seat of the Godhead. A flaming door appeared in the middle of the tent and the Father stepped in. He sat down to judge, with the Son of God at His right hand.

The kings and lords were judged first. Those who ruled with cruelty and darkness were banished forever because the love the Father and the Son had for the earth and for the sons of men would not be brought through the fire a second time. Those who ruled in the Spirit of Holiness and by the Father's love and wisdom were given vast cities and regions to steward. They immediately went out to raise up tents in these areas, and began to judge and restore the regions entrusted to them forever. It was necessary to judge the kings and lords first so they could prepare the place where all of those who followed could live after they had been rewarded. It was impossible for anyone to enter into these cities and regions without first passing through these tents of judgement to be sure they would fit there.

Next came the worshippers and entertainers. Those who sought to glorify themselves and released perversion through the music, movies, and art they produced were banished forever because the Father would not allow such things a second time. But those who sought to bless and beautify others and glorify the Father were sent to bless and beautify every city and region on the earth. I was surprised that some "Christian" entertainers were banished and some "secular" entertainers rewarded, and took this as a warning to be careful about any assumptions concerning the Father's judgements. For example, some movie directors were greatly rewarded for faithfully releasing messages from the Father to the masses, while some Christian entertainers wept in the outer darkness for sacrificing their gifts at the shallow altars of money and self-promotion. They wept because they now saw with clarity the power and beauty of what *could have been* released through them if they had sought the Lord instead of self-promotion. They were saved "as one escaping through the flames," but took their place among the least.

Next came the prophets, teachers, and shepherds. Once again, I was surprised because many of those who faithfully stewarded these mantles were never recognized on earth but received a great reward here. Likewise, some of the most famous names wept in the outer darkness because of what *could have been* released through them if they had sought the Lord's close fellowship instead of men's praise. They too were saved, but also were assigned a place among the least.

When the mature priesthood came, they faced no judgement by the Father and the Son and they faced no judgement from the kings and lords—for they had already *judged themselves* with the penetrating light of His eyes. They had already walked in such close fellowship with the Father, drinking His fine wines and choice meats, that they already *knew* what He thought about them and made daily changes until they perfectly fulfilled what was written about them in heaven. They had already lived lives of close partnership and mutual blessing with the leaders the Father had chosen. And so, when the mature priesthood came onto the scene, it was a day like no other.

The mature priesthood came with a basin of pure water, to wash everyone's feet with tears of love. They came with the light of the lampstand on their shoulders, to give everyone a glimpse of what still lay ahead in the ages to come. They came with a fragrant incense altar, which now shown as a bright star of all the accumulated prayers from all of time. They came with a table of showbread, to release the weighty thoughts of God to all of humanity. And they came with the ark, and a clear declaration that *this* was to be the ultimate resting place of the Father's throne forever and ever.

As each mature priest approached the Lord, the Lord took him into his belly. At that moment, a stone would appear in the holy city *and* a star would appear in the heavens. In this way, the holy city rose to take shape and the heavens greatly increased in brightness as each hour of the long day progressed.

As each group came before Father and Son, the whole assembly could *see* what they were thinking and feeling. They could *see* their hearts breaking when one had to be banished to the place where the powers of darkness were confined. They could feel the weight of emotion as people saw what *could have been* or felt the delight of God in their faithfulness. In this way, even the hours of judgement became a procession of worship, as the people began to rejoice and mourn along with Father and Son, held together with them in an unbroken circle of fellowship, wisdom, and love. I saw unreached people groups from throughout time, those who never had the light of the gospel, but there were many among them who had read God's *second book*—the witness of creation—and longed for a Messiah whose name they did not know. Now, the full redemption of Christ was applied to them in accordance with how they had learned to abide in His love. I was reminded of the Father's declaration to Moses—

"I will have mercy on whomever I will have mercy, and I will have compassion on whomever I will have compassion" (Romans 9:15 NKJV).

It was not a declaration of universalism, but a declaration of the Father's unrestrained sovereignty. Only *He* had the full resources at His disposal to judge each one properly. Others of the unready people, who had read the *second book* and chose the depths of depravity and cruelty, were swiftly banished. Here, the Father and Son separated all of them with love, clarity, and justice. It was not possible for anyone to lay an accusation against the judgements of the Father or the Son in that place, for they could see with perfection the wisdom behind every decision and they cried out together—

"We give You thanks, O Lord God Almighty, the One who is and who was and who is to come, because You have taken Your great power and reigned.

The nations were angry, and Your wrath has come, and the time of the dead, that they should be judged, and that You should reward Your servants the prophets and the saints, and those who fear Your name, small and great, and should destroy those who destroy the earth" (Revelation 11:17-18).

As they said it, for some reason I saw in my mind's eye the Father's horse again, eating the grass on the Father's lawn. But now the grass was growing *here* because the Father's tent was raised up as a permanent habitation on the earth. I wondered what He could possibly be preparing for after all of these things. The Father's horse spoke:

Whether the journey goes up—or plunges low,
My quest is still the same,
to simply be a seat for Him
In glory or in pain.

My quest is to be with Him

Through all of time and space
That I may feed more deeply
from the light that's in His face.

I looked at him long time, contemplating what he was and who it was He carried. And I spoke softly, as the restorative wind rustled new leaves in golden trees and songbirds sang with notes beyond what had been heard before on the earth—

"Yes...that's *my* quest too."

OTHER BOOKS BY MICHAEL FICKESS

DEVOTIONALS AND THEOLOGICAL WORKS

Enoch's Blessing

Paths of Ever-Increasing Glory

The Rise of His Holy Ones

The CSCL Bible Curriculum Series

Restoring the Apostolic Gospel

PROPHETIC ALLEGORIES

Start the Countdown

The Restoration of All Things

Other titles in The Great Acceleration Trilogy

Designed to impart a balance of Word and Spirit.

This unique series of Bible studies is designed to help disciple students, church discipleship groups, and the multitudes of new believers who will come to the Lord as the next move of God unfolds. To learn more, download free sample lessons, or purchase, please visit:

http://mstarm.us/bible

Made in the USA
Middletown, DE
28 December 2018